T0302077

Hearing the Voice of the Shingo Principles

Creating Sustainable Cultures of Enterprise Excellence

Hearing the Voice of the Shingo Principles

Creating Sustainable Cultures of Enterprise Excellence

Robert D. Miller

Routledge
Taylor & Francis Group

A PRODUCTIVITY PRESS BOOK

Routledge
Taylor & Francis Group
711 Third Avenue, New York, NY 10017

© 2018 by Robert D. Miller
Productivity Press is an imprint of Taylor & Francis Group, an Informa business

No claim to original U.S. Government works

Printed on acid-free paper

International Standard Book Number-13: 978-0-8153-8704-6 (Hardback)
International Standard Book Number-13: 978-1-351-17400-8 (eBook)

Visit the Taylor & Francis Web site at
http://www.taylorandfrancis.com

and the Productivity Press site at
http://www.ProductivityPress.com

Contents

Preface

Native American lore often talks of how different elements of nature speak with a voice. A wise person learns to listen to the voice of the wind, the sun, the trees, the rivers, etc. In business we often speak of the voice of the shareholders, the voice of the employees and the voice of the customers. Successful leaders learn to listen to each of these voices and develop powerful management systems that respond to them.

Principles also have a voice. These are the natural laws that govern the success of all of our business and organizational ventures. Principles speak the truth all day long, every day. Principles never take vacations or become irrelevant. Principles govern our results whether or not we pay attention to them. They shout to the person who has learned to listen and are mute to those who tune them out. The most successful people through the ages are those who are intimately familiar with the voice of principles and have become what we might call "principled."

This book is about learning to listen to the voice of a principle. When we hear the voice of a principle, it informs us about how to act that will create the most positive outcome. When we fail to or are unable to hear the voice of a principle we disregard perhaps the most critical component of organizational or even personal strategy. Since the voice of a principle informs ideal behaviors, a discussion of principles becomes also a discussion about organizational culture.

This book is intended to help its readers learn to hear the voice of guiding principles in the creation of sustainable cultures of enterprise excellence.

For more information or to leave your comments on the book please visit either: http://archesleadership.com/ or http://hearing thevoiceoftheshingoprinciples.com

Acknowledgments

My thanks go out to the countless, incredible people who have served as role models for me over many years. Their patience, support and belief in me have been a continual source of inspiration for personal growth.

I am deeply grateful for the many companies that have allowed me to become a part of their operations in some small way. When they asked for feedback I appreciate their willingness to be vulnerable so that I could express my observations without censorship.

To Margo, my wonderful wife of 44 years, goes my deepest love and appreciation. She never let me give up on my desire for many years to write this book. She never once let the project get too far on to the back burner. When I returned full of great stories from an amazing visit to a client, or some other great organization, she would say, "Robert, that needs to be a part of your book!"

I am grateful to my children and their equally amazing spouses, who even busy with their own children and careers, found time to critically review my work. I see much of their mother's influence in their independent spirits that gave them the courage to tell me the truth about what might make the book better.

A special thanks to my son Brock who, late at night after work and after his children were in bed, spent many hours providing incredibly insightful feedback on many of the chapters. The evolution of his questions helped me to determine whether or not I was explaining an idea clearly.

My thanks to Utah State University and the Shingo Prize for providing the support needed for development of the Shingo Model in the basement offices of the student dormitory cafeteria, right below the deep fat fryer.... It was great, but maybe a bit hard on my waistline!

Finally, I am forever grateful to God, whom I believe has planted in each of us an innate recognition of truth and principles. I almost always feel that people hear the ideas presented in this book not just with their ears or even with their heads, but more importantly, with their hearts.

Author

Robert D. Miller is the lead architect and thought leader of the Shingo Model. This model is a breakthrough approach to leadership based on rigorously integrating a few key principles of behavior into all of the management systems of an enterprise.

Robert has extensive global experience in top management, public service, higher education, and consulting in both large and small organizations. Unique stories included in this book bring to reality the positive impact of principles in every enterprise and workplace.

Mr. Miller invites his readers to deeply consider each principle, appropriately apply them into their own style of management and begin to experience a positive transformation in the engagement of associates, improvement in results and create a sustainable culture of excellence.

Mr. Miller led the Shingo Institute at Utah State University and was inducted into the Shingo Academy in 2014. Robert and his wife Margo have been married for 44 years. They have five children, 18 grandchildren and live in Northern Utah.

Visit www.archesleadership.com. Arches Leadership is an Advisory Service and a Licensed Affiliate of the Shingo Institute at Utah State University.

Introduction

In 1976 I was employed as a manufacturing engineer at the John Deere Harvester Works plant in East Moline, Illinois. I was young, naïve and a bit overwhelmed coming from a small agricultural community in southern Alberta, now to a nearly two million square foot factory employing many hundreds of people. It was a time of abundance in the agricultural industry and I was one of dozens of new engineers hired from some of the great engineering schools in the USA.

Searching for a way to excel and differentiate myself, I became fascinated by the emergence of computers in many factories as a way to improve quality and increase productivity. Deep in the winter of 1976 I was given permission to attend a weeklong workshop at the University of Wisconsin in Madison on the workings and programming of a microprocessor. At the conclusion of the week, I was certain of three things. One, I had no interest or aptitude for computer or software design; two, I knew that nothing in the world of manufacturing would ever be the same and three, and perhaps most importantly, that successfully implementing this technology into the workplace would take far more than computer scientists; it would take exceptional leadership and an approach to management that involved and engaged every worker in a fundamentally different way, both in the office and on the factory floor.

In 1977 I was given a leave of absence from Deere & Company to return to university as a candidate for a Master's of Science degree in Computer-Integrated Manufacturing, an emerging new field of study. Unlike others more technically inclined, my thesis research was *Management Style and Computer-Aided Manufacturing: A Correlation Study.**

Results of the study showed eight specific aspects of management style that had a significant correlation with performance of Computer-Aided Manufacturing (CAM) Systems.

They were:

1. Decisions should reflect long-range company goals and strategy.
2. Superiors should have a good understanding of problems faced by subordinates who are actually involved in the problems.

---

* M.S. Degree, 1978, Brigham Young University, Robert D. Miller.

3. Management must be well prepared for decision-making.
4. Actual users should be highly involved in the initial system design.
5. Projects must be well integrated with all possible departments.
6. Subordinates should be making a substantial contribution to the decision-making process.
7. Rewards and involvement should be used as much as possible as motivators.
8. There should be complete cooperation between all levels of management.*

Looking back, I am amazed at how the key insights gained from that research in 1978 ignited a spark that has guided my career over the last 40 years and in no small way fanned the flame that has compelled me to write this book. I am struck by how similar they are to many of the things written about in this book. Telling my stories and sharing my insights has helped me to recognize the progression of life experiences that contributed to development of what we now call the "Shingo Model."

While working for FMC Corporation in Chicago, Illinois, I began focusing on the implementation of Computer-Aided Design (CAD) systems but soon found myself focusing on the ideas of Material Requirements Planning (MRP), Total Quality Management (TQM) and Just-in-time (JIT) manufacturing. No surprise that my experiences around the world with this company led me to the same conclusions as my Master's thesis: that the greatest impact on the successes of these technical ideas was not the technology, but the people who were implementing and using it.

As Vice President of Manufacturing Engineering at Herman Miller, Inc. in Zeeland, Michigan, I was captivated by the title they gave to the leader of the Human Resource department, Vice President "For People." Herman Miller, Inc., then led by Max DePree, an unusually visionary leader, exemplified a deep and personal commitment to the people who produced their excellent, high design, office furniture products.

I participated in a two-year leadership development experience encouraged by the company that consisted of four weeklong retreats, separated by six months. At these sessions, the outside facilitator created experiences for us to lead to a deep appreciation for what was called by Carl Rogers, as the "Person Centered Approach," or PCA. He applied it to clinical

* "Management Style Recommendations" pg. 62–67 RD Miller Thesis, 1978.

psychology, but we applied it to business. PCA was based on three key concepts: Congruence, Empathy and Unconditional Positive Regard. All three concepts were about people and how we interact with each other in a way that demonstrates humility and respect. To me, it was amazing that I found myself employed by a company that felt that the highest form of development for its leaders had less to do with technical competence and everything to do with how we interacted with and enabled the potential of its people.

Circumstances led me to Denver, Colorado, where I was hired by the Gates Rubber Company, largely to help them shore up their culture. Gates was a privately held company formed just after the turn of the century. For over 90 years, two generations of Gates patriarchs led the company. Their pioneering work ethic symbolized for employees the company's commitment to family, self-determination, initiative and overcoming whatever obstacles may emerge in the pathway to progress. A symbol of this commitment was found in a metaphor they called the *Hat in Hand*.

This symbol was based on the old pioneer practice where the father, upon arriving at a creek or river, leapt from the seat of his wagon, took off his favorite hat and with all his might, threw it across the creek (Figure I.1). Everyone in the family knew that no self-respecting pioneer would think of leaving his favorite hat behind, so the hat on the far side of the creek became a symbol to his family that nothing will stop us from getting across this creek and retrieving Dad's hat. This story became a symbol of the pioneering spirit and supportive culture of the company.

Over the years, as the company grew and managers were hired and eventually retired, many of the long-held values of the family owners were lost from the play-book of daily management behaviors. Little by little, frontline workers at the factory closest to the headquarters concluded that the best way to protect themselves from perceived one-sided management policies was to organize into a collective bargaining unit.

Predictably, rather than solving the problem, this action led to even greater barriers between management and labor. Trust was lost, commitment to improvement evaporated and ultimately, years later, the mother-plant was closed, hundreds of jobs were lost, families uprooted and service to customers severely affected.

My assignment from Charlie Gates, as we all fondly referred to him, who would soon be retiring, was to help him return the company to the culture that it was once built on.

Throw Your Hat Across The Creek

FIGURE I.1
"Throw Your Hat Across The Creek," the symbol representing early values of the Gates Rubber Company.

This assignment opened my eyes to many of the insights I will share in this book. From this experience, I became keenly interested in the formation and transformation of corporate culture. During the years that I served as a member of the Gates Executive Board of Management, I gained critical insights that informed my thinking, beliefs and personal behaviors in many profound ways.

Additionally, important to Mr. Gates was that his executives be engaged in some meaningful way to support the local communities where we worked. I chose to become affiliated with and eventually became the Chairman of the Board for a not-for-profit group called the Denver Public Education and Business Coalition. Our mission was to engage businesses in supporting local school districts. At one of the school districts I worked closely with, we attempted to implement the criteria of the Malcolm Baldrige National Quality Award, recently updated for application into an academic setting. After nearly two years of effort we found that while the criteria defined in the Baldrige Award was clearly applicable; teachers in the schools were continuously constrained by the management practices and culture created by school and district administrators and even local and state boards of education. Culture again trumped everything else.

Freshly inspired by my experiences, I became a partner in a consulting firm in Boulder, Colorado, specializing in the implementation of continuous improvement programs. Our specialty was teaching leaders how to pay as much attention to building acceptance for their great ideas as they did for the idea itself. We ascribed to the formula: $E = Q^*A$, which came from the General Electric Company's work on Change Acceleration. The formula represented the concept that the Effectiveness (E) of any initiative is a function of the Quality (Q) of the technical solution multiplied by the Acceptance (A) of the idea by the people. Later we evolved the formula to reflect what we observed over and over: that the relationship between Q and A is not linear but rather exponential. The Q and the A are not equal. A suboptimal solution, implemented into a supportive, empowered and engaged workforce will usually create a far better outcome than the perfect Q implemented with little or no regard for the people who are required to make it work—another affirmation of my now lifelong observations about organizational culture.

In the years since my Master's degree thesis, I have worked with great organizations and closely affiliated with a broad mix of leaders and managers. From some, I observed behaviors that helped me to decide with great clarity and commitment what I would never do. From others, I have been deeply inspired, vowing that I would strive throughout my life to demonstrate personal attributes as close to theirs as possible. Of course, I have also learned much through my own numerous mistakes and occasional successes.

In 2006, the latter phase of my professional career, I found myself in academia at Utah State University where I was asked to become a part of a very successful industrial recognition program called the Shingo Prize inside the Business School. The Shingo Prize was a recognition program created in 1986 by Professor Vern Buehler, Norman Bodek and others at the Jon M. Huntsman School of Business. The initial vision was that by identifying and recognizing great organizations that demonstrated exemplary application of the tools of continuous improvement, others would become motivated to improve. I became executive director of the Shingo Prize in 2007.

Knowing that a prize is only valued if it represents something of great worth, my team began a study to understand what the reality was concerning the *value* of the Shingo Prize. What we learned was identical to what I had been experiencing since 1978 and provided a giant wakeup call for what we must do next.

We learned that meeting the technical requirements of the Prize was only minimally predictive of the company's ability to sustain excellence over the long term. What became clear was that a trophy in the lobby was only as valuable as the real world behind the front doors.

Studying the feedback given to applicants for the Prize, observing past recipients and a broad engagement of thought leaders all over the world eventually led us to the development of a model from which we could evaluate and reliably predict the sustainability of an organization's improvements once receiving the recognition. Not surprisingly, the new criteria, based on what we called "The Shingo Model,"* was far less technical than it was focused on the behaviors of leaders, managers and frontline associates throughout the entire enterprise. We found that we were predicting the long-term success of the business based on our assessment of their culture.

This bar was substantially more difficult for applicant companies to measure up to, but rather than leading to the demise of the Shingo Prize, as many predicted, it led to an exponential increase in global interest in our new and lofty standard. What we developed, was a worldwide recognition that every effort to make improvements, of any kind, were based less on the technical merits of the strategy than they were on the culture of the organization into which the strategy is introduced. Even though for most, changing organizational culture seemed almost impossible, companies were attracted to the realization that their ideal results required the creation of a great organizational culture.

As demand for understanding how to transform corporate culture based on the Shingo Model grew, it became clear that giving the Prize was secondary to our research and education, and the Shingo Institute at Utah State University was born. This meant a far deeper analysis on how to best teach the many key concepts built into the Shingo Model (Figure I.2). What I thought would be easily explained has instead taken me personally on a lengthy search to explain these Shingo Model concepts in a way that they can be understood and acted on.

---

* IP owned by Utah State University.

FIGURE I.2
Chief architects of the Shingo Model. Shown from left: Shaun Barker, Randy Cook, Robert Miller (Team Lead), and Jacob Raymer (2015).

I retired from the Shingo Institute at Utah State University in July of 2014 and created Arches Leadership, a private consulting group and Shingo Institute licensed affiliate to teach the Shingo Model licensed courses* and consultancy. Privately, I could focus more closely on the companies that were earnestly and genuinely committed to a compelling journey of fundamentally reshaping their corporate culture. These are the companies that understand that the success of all of their strategic initiatives is ultimately based on their creating a sustainable culture of enterprise excellence.

It has taken many years for me to think somewhat naturally and spontaneously through the lenses that will be described in the following chapters. For this work to achieve its intended purpose, I invite each of you to embark on a similar journey of your own.

I am not suggesting to any reader that their goal be to simply "Implement the Shingo Model." Rather, the goal might be to use the Model to facilitate reshaping your thinking and beliefs about what is most important for leaders to be engaged in.

I encourage you to read this book slowly and thoughtfully. Many new ideas and insights will be presented that are best understood after reflection and discussion with your colleagues. It may be best if several co-workers

---

* IP owned by USU.

read the book simultaneously. Your collaborators should be those who will help you to see "reality."

"Creating Sustainable Cultures of Enterprise Excellence" will be the most challenging work you will ever do. It will also be the most rewarding!

Reader's Guide to Learning: Trying to teach many of the ideas introduced in subsequent chapters requires more learning than just the chapter the idea is introduced in. Try keeping notes of your questions on topics that seem more complex than what you understood. In each chapter I have tried to build on what was discussed previously, so be patient and don't give up if you don't think that you fully understand an idea when it is introduced. I have shared many stories and experiences throughout but recommend you find your own stories and share them with others as a way to relate to each topic.

Good luck and good reading!

Robert Miller

1

The Power of the Culture

Most organizational cultures are not built purposefully; they simply emerge while we are busy focusing on results.

Listening to the daily onslaught of stories on the television and radio of how great companies and organizations are being systematically destroyed from the inside by the behavior of their leaders is disheartening. Many of these institutions are critical to our sustainability as a society and include state and federal governments, news organizations, police and military institutions and corporations both large and small.

Sadly, the egregious behaviors we are forced to hear about rarely represent a singular instance but almost always reflect a deeply entrenched culture of power, ego, disrespect, intolerance, mediocrity, sexual impropriety and even corruption. The private and public demonstration of these behaviors affects everyone and everything they touch. The many good people inside of these organizations are deeply affected by and even tainted by the examples of their leaders. The culture of the organization is very often the source of the disease that ultimately destroys the organism.

Every time I think we have heard the worst of it something new and even worse is reported. We see the establishment of good laws to protect and preserve the sanctity of people, sacrificed by a culture where listening for understanding is seen as a sign of weakness and compromise to find win/win solutions is seen as flip-flopping. Ideal results are sacrificed every day on the altar of a culture of winning, no matter what it takes or at what cost. The consequences of such public demonstrations of a culture turned toxic can be seen inside almost any organization and at almost any level.

Organizational culture is rarely discussed seriously or strategically in the context of conducting business. The pursuit of results consumes the minds and calendars of nearly every leader and manager in every organization, leaving very little energy for softer topics like culture. Occasionally an exceptional leader arises who naturally sees the relationship between results and behavior or culture but for the rest of us discussions of culture happen almost exclusively in the Human Resources Department.

Conversations about culture and ideal behaviors in the workplace seem to have been largely replaced by efforts to provide fully stocked kitchens, unlimited amounts of caffeine on tap, very casual dress codes, beach cruisers and hover boards in the office to get from place to place, even a slide between floors, gymnasiums, ping pong tables, on-site massage therapists, on-site child care, unlimited paid time off, very flexible work hours, working from home (or wherever), free golf and ski passes and most recently, pets coming to work with their owners (to relieve stress). It seems that companies compete for employees by trying to out-perk their competitors and call it a "great place to work."

In my conversations with many of the people (mostly young) who work in these companies, after describing the benefits, go on to share stories of what it is like to do the actual work. One of them recently observed soberly; "Yes we like the perks, but if people don't like their boss, they end up only working for the perks and just put up with the work." This person actually then said, "No amount of ping pong can make up for a bad work culture."

As important as these social perks have become, the real culture of an organization is far more than that. As in Figure 1.1, perks are like the tip of the iceberg that you see above the water. The full measure of organizational culture is the part that is below the surface and is very difficult to see, but is ultimately reflected in every aspect of every employee's work.

Employees often report that a relatively small percentage of the employees actually use most of the perks provided but every single employee is deeply impacted by the part of the culture that has to do with the way work gets done, the part below the surface. This is the part of work where strategy, plans and decisions get made, people collaborate on projects, problems get identified and solved and customers are provided with great products and services. This is the part of work that can be deeply satisfying or profoundly frustrating.

This book is directed not to the "perk" based part of the culture above the surface, the ten percent, but to the hidden work-related part

FIGURE 1.1
The "perk" culture vs. the total culture. (By license.)

of the culture, the 90 percent. This is the part of the culture where principles should speak most loudly and help to inform every single associate, no matter their level or responsibility, about how best to act to maximize both personal contribution and satisfaction and organizational effectiveness.

THE DE FACTO CULTURE

The creation of a high performing work culture within any organization may have the greatest single impact on the organization's ability to create great results of anything a leader can do. Unfortunately, building a sustainable culture of excellence is also the hardest thing that a leader will ever do. Creating a great culture is not something that can be delegated or purchased; it requires a deep personal commitment to people and a daily genuine demonstration of ideal behaviors. Building a sustainable culture of excellence is not for the faint of heart; it requires a sustained commitment over many years and a complete realignment of virtually every management and work system in the organization. As hard as it is, creating and sustaining a culture of excellence will also likely be the most rewarding thing you will ever do in the context of your profession.

As hard as it is, creating and sustaining a culture of excellence will likely be the most rewarding thing you will ever do in the context of your profession.

Typically, the culture that emerges while everyone is focusing on results is what I call a "de facto" culture. De facto cultures are not intentionally designed; rather, they are the consequence of many small and a few large decisions made over a very long period of time. What emerges on its own as organizational culture ultimately has a profound impact on the behavioral choices made by every single person, top to bottom and side to side. How people behave in any organization may be the greatest single determinant on the quality and sustainability of results. A de facto culture rarely has the capacity to deliver ideal results over the long term.

A de facto culture rarely has the capacity to deliver ideal results over the long term.

From my discussions with literally thousands of leaders in a host of organizations and industries, I have observed that creating a relentless and enterprise-wide focus on the achievement of business performance metrics, or "results" has become the prevailing mindset for achieving success. This almost singular focus from senior management teams drives the thinking, strategies and behaviors of the entire enterprise. All of the organizational energy becomes focused 24/7 on the achievement of business results; almost everything else becomes subordinate to that one aim. Even actions directed at supporting people are usually motivated by how this action will contribute to the achievement of better business results.

Most of the people I have worked with to build a sustainable culture of excellence start with the question, "How can focusing on results be a bad thing?" In fact, it is not a bad thing; but if it becomes the singular focus, it leaves to chance the evolution of the corporate culture and rarely does what emerges have the capacity to generate ideal and sustainable results over the long term.

The unspoken and often-unintended consequence of this relentless focus on results is a culture of "results at any cost!" Certainly leaders never intend to say, "Get it done at any cost." Most would be horrified to even imagine anyone thinking they actually meant, "at any cost."

I recently worked with a group of mostly middle managers who, when confronting this part of their culture, confessed in hushed tones and only when the door was closed that "Even though our leaders don't say it, we all know exactly what they mean; 'Don't tell me how you did it, just get it done.'"

Rob Galloway, President of US Synthetic, says it this way; "Sometimes we get so focused on results that we will do anything to get them and we forget that the approach we take will have a cultural impact. Every leadership decision is a culture decision." Each time we choose to act or leave to chance the way that others act in the pursuit of great results, we have an impact on the culture of the organization.

> *Sometimes we get so focused on results that we will do anything to get them and we forget that the approach we take will have a cultural impact. Every leadership decision is a culture decision.*
>
> **Rob Galloway**
> *President, US Synthetic*

My hat does go off to associates who even in the face of a less than perfect culture are able to deliver good results. What a leader must ask him or herself is, "Is this sustainable? How long can I keep asking people to go through what they must to keep getting things done? I wonder what more our people could do if they had a better environment in which to do it? What are the unseen consequences of allowing and perhaps even encouraging people to behave the way they do in pursuit of results?"

THE COST OF BAD BEHAVIOR

Can great results that deliver value for customers be achieved with bad behavior? Nearly everyone I have ever asked this question to, answers it in the same way; "Yes of course you can; we do it all the time!" Naturally my next question is, "Yes, but is it sustainable, and at what cost?"

The cost of striving to achieve ideal results with consistently bad behavior is enormous. These costs, both financial and non-financial, are reflected in the following symptoms that flow from bad organizational behavior.

1. Unexpected or inexplicable problems
2. Low productivity
3. Low morale
4. A lack of innovation

5. Long workdays for managers
6. Bloated staff
7. Significant, sustained and unplanned overtime for employees
8. Constant fire fighting
9. High turnover
10. Frequent customer disappointments

Consider in your own organization the *total cost* of these symptoms. What is the impact on your organization of low morale, lack of innovation, constant fire fighting, high turnover of personnel and customer disappointments? While these outcomes are not usually measured on a balance sheet; most leaders, managers and even frontline workers can easily describe in great detail from what they see every day what the impact these unresolved "cultural indicators" have on the results of the company.

I once was asked to perform an organizational assessment for a company that was experiencing a 40% turnover of its employees each year, yet just up the road another company in a similar industry experienced almost no turnover. The cost and disruption caused by this lack of commitment was enormous. Serious quality issues led to a near total collapse of their business in a vitally important industry.

The team leader's and senior management response to the crises was almost completely technical. Greater controls, tighter specifications, improved documentation, automation and more inspection were among the solutions being implemented. These solutions were almost exclusively a top-down design. Their implementation fundamentally changed the way that almost every worker did their jobs. To their credit, senior management also invested in a nicer cafeteria, beautiful landscaping, an exercise room available to all employees for a nominal fee and higher base salaries, mostly perks.

I spent two days on the floor talking to as many people as I could to better understand what it was like to work in this organization. My experiences were deeply moving. I met some of the most wonderful and committed employees I have ever had the pleasure of meeting. I found them to be highly educated, humble, respectful, deeply committed to the quality of what they did and highly supportive of each other. I also learned that they came from many different countries and that for many, English was a distant second language.

In a conversation with an incredible lady from Central America, she was very eager to describe the work that she did. It was extremely intricate and critical to the quality of the product that would ultimately end up in the human body keeping someone alive. As she described her work, tears came to her eyes when she told me how she felt about knowing that what she did would become so intimately a part of another human being. After drying my own eyes I asked her about her tears. She told me that many times during the day she found herself emotional from thinking about the lives and families of people who would be changed because of what she did.

I was naturally drawn to her and wanted to know more about who she was. With a little prodding I discovered that she had a college degree in Accounting, but when she came to America her degree was not recognized and so she was forced to take the only position she could get, which was in production. A smile then crossed her face and she said, "But you should meet my two friends who I work with!" She then turned to the ladies on her right and on her left. One was a nurse and the other a schoolteacher, both from two different countries!

While I was thinking about how sad it was that they were not working in the fields in which they were trained, all three of them said; "But our greatest disappointment in our work here is not being asked to become involved in the many ways we see to make our work better."

On and on people from all over the operations told me that they felt like little more than a "pair of hands" while the people with the "brains" all came from the engineering and management ranks. Solutions to the critical quality problems of the company were largely being imposed on them, often making their jobs more difficult. No one ever asked or enabled them to contribute their expertise to the job of making things better.

Now, consider the *total cost* to the company of their failure to acknowledge and leverage the full capabilities and potential of these three exceptional people. These just happened to be the three I was able to meet. Imagine the lost value of the entire workforce of more than 200 other good people, each with great intrinsic value and enormous untapped potential.

If you are a leader or manager working in an environment where focusing solely on results or the technical solutions to problems affecting the results, you are probably under too much pressure to notice the impact this leadership behavior has on the behaviors of everyone else in the organization.

The ideal results that leaders most often seek are those that maximize customer value creation and are sustainable over the long term. These kinds of results can only be achieved with ideal behaviors from every employee.

It has been very disappointing to see so many leaders fail to recognize the profound impact they unknowingly have on corporate culture and the often-negative impact that these cultures have on the results they work so hard to achieve. No matter how neglected corporate culture may be, by expanding leadership focus from simply results to both results *and* behavior (culture), a leader can fundamentally change the trajectory of any organization and create a great legacy. At the end of your professional working life, you will no doubt remember the technical achievements you may have made but you will remember with great fondness the lives you touched and enabled through your leadership. Any financial success you created will likely pale when compared.

> *At the end of your professional working life, you will most likely remember with great fondness the lives you enabled through your leadership. Any financial success you created will likely pale when compared.*

CULTURE'S IMPACT ON RESULTS

Perhaps the most important question then for every leader is: "If I must deliver ideal and sustainable results, and I must; what are *all* of the factors that I must focus the organization on that will give us the greatest probability of delivering great results?"

It is the premise of this work, that organizational culture, or the collective understanding of how people should and do act, that has the greatest impact on the achievement of results. Culture is the cause leading to great results, the effect. Further, creating a high performing culture is the most important work that any leader will ever do.

> *The only thing of real importance that leaders do is to create and manage culture. If you do not manage culture, it manages you, and you may not even be aware of the extent to which this is happening.*

> **Edgar Schein**
> *Professor MIT Sloan School of Management*

To lead culture, leaders must understand what causes people to behave the way they do. We will explore this question in greater detail in subsequent chapters.

One common definition of culture is, "The sum of all learned and socially demonstrated patterns of behavior." In a company where I was hired with the express purpose of restoring the culture to a bygone era, my peers said; "Bob, you've only got six months to get this done...after that you'll have become one of us," meaning the culture will have swallowed you up and your own patterns of behavior will have conformed to what people have learned to do to "get things done around here." It is often said that, "Culture eats strategy for breakfast."

Each of us have had our own experience at learning how to "get things done" in whatever situations we have found ourselves. We are invited to or perhaps excluded from the coffee klatches before work, we adopt certain behaviors in meetings, we create monthly reports in a certain format, we learn where to park, how early to show up and when it's OK to go home. We learn who has the power, how to influence them and who to avoid. We learn what is required to get ahead and what behavior will no doubt be the "kiss of death."

Little by little and in a hundred small ways, we learn the patterns of behavior that represent the culture. For most, our success or failure is largely determined by our ability to understand the culture and work within it. People who cannot or refuse to conform with the culture usually find themselves isolated and on the outside. Over time, most people who exist outside the prevailing culture of an organization are not successful. They are either asked to leave or become so uncomfortable that they choose to leave of their own free will.

I worked with a man once who joined our company as a Senior Vice President. He had a military background and had worked for a company known for its rigorous and dictatorial culture of top-down management control. How he got to our company is still somewhat of a mystery. Our culture was very open, collaborative and highly participative at all levels. Almost all decisions were made at the lowest level possible.

For a while, I wondered if someone at the top of our company had decided we were going the wrong direction and had intentionally placed this person into a position of leadership because they wanted the culture to change. I watched with great interest, wondering whether the forceful personality of the new SVP would win out or the culture of our company would eventually overwhelm even him.

For a while, everyone was confused. In an apparent effort to support the new executive it seemed that every month a story about what he was doing was on the front page of our company newsletter. Behind the scenes however, his approach to decision-making and communications was building a growing wall of resentment. It took over a year, but eventually the people from inside the culture became like antibodies protecting the organism from something entirely foreign to it and the power of the culture won out and he left.

HOW WE DESCRIBE CULTURE

We often describe cultures in different ways. We may describe a culture as being toxic. It may be described as bureaucratic, "good ol' boy," paternal, innovative or perhaps maybe even respectful. Each conjures up in our minds a whole set of behaviors that are likely to be found inside of that organization.

For example, a "toxic" culture is a culture where people are afraid to tell the truth, to get engaged or to take a risk. It is one where everyone watches their own backs and acts in their own self-interest rather than in the best interest of others, the organization or the customer. The outcomes of a toxic culture are employees who are afraid to take risks for fear of being wrong. Creativity is stifled, employee turnover is high and instead of bringing out the best in people it brings out the worst in them. Ultimately a toxic culture breeds a disease that eventually kills the organism.

A "good ol' boy" culture is one that values the long-term relationships of a few people who have become a part of the key network of influencers in the company. People not a part of the "club" find themselves on the outside with little influence on decisions or actions that are taken. The outcomes of this culture are often an inbreeding of like-minded thinkers, people who feel powerless to influence change and either give up and leave or give up and stay.

> *The outcomes of a good ol' boy culture are often an inbreeding of like-minded thinkers, people who feel powerless to influence change and either give up and leave or give up and stay.*

A culture of respect is one that values the individual contributions and potential of every associate. People tell the truth, take reasonable risks and support the development of others. Some of the outcomes of this culture are the retention of good workers, continuous improvement and corporate growth.

ARTIFACTS AND CULTURE

Cultures manifest themselves in many different ways. Archeologists study the cultures of ancient civilizations by excavating the physical remnants of the people. From the locations, layout and the design of buildings, inferences can be drawn about how the people lived together and the degree of knowledge they possessed. From personal items that are found they can infer their degree of wealth, roles in society, who they traded with, what they ate and even the nature of family life. Artifacts can be physically observed. They tell stories about the people who possessed them, what they valued and ultimately, the culture of the people.

Our homes and communities are filled with artifacts that similarly tell stories about the people who live in them. Parks, playgrounds, athletic fields, shopping malls, churches, synagogues and even billboards reveal much about the culture of a community. Our homes have pictures, family heirlooms, work charts for children, musical instruments, sports equipment and maybe even an antique car. From each, an inference can be made about the people who live in the home and collectively, they tell a story about the culture of the family.

Similarly, our factories and offices are filled with artifacts that tell stories about the culture of the people who work in them. What hangs on the office walls and cubicles not only tells us about the people who occupy them, but also what is most important to the company itself. The layout of machinery, the kind of information displayed for/by the workers, the presence or absence of recognition for people's contributions or the proximity of workstations relative to peers or supervisors. These artifacts are the tangible evidence of how the company thinks about the people who do the work that creates value for customers.

What leaders value the most becomes evident in corporate artifacts. I once worked where the senior executives had their own private parking garage. The CEO had an elevator that took him straight to his office so he didn't have to accidentally bump into an employee. Another large company I worked for once had a beautifully adorned executive dining room that was off-limits to anyone below a certain pay grade.

On the other hand, I once visited a company that had a beautiful walking track around a pond for all employees, one company had an exercise gym for all employees, another had a beautiful cafeteria for all employees with healthy meals subsidized by the company.

All of these examples are the physical evidence of what a company values the most. Each value and its associated artifact had either a positive or negative impact on the behaviors of employees and ultimately their results. An organization that values people and relationships is likely to have on its walls pictures of people recognizing others and being recognized for important contributions, announcements of the upcoming picnic or the birth of a new baby. If they value teams, the pictures will likely be of smiling groups of people obviously proud of some goal they achieved together.

On the walls of an organization that is focused almost exclusively on the work and the results, you might see things like memos on policy, work schedules and scorecards showing monthly results. Information is shared in a format primarily intended to communicate whether or not the people had *made the numbers.*

I worked in a company once that had a strong and genuine respect for every single employee. One of the ways they demonstrated that respect was to design their facilities so that every worker had the ability to work in natural light from the outside. One of my responsibilities included management of the facilities, so I knew how much extra money the company had to spend to build factories and offices where natural light reached every corner of the workspace. The buildings and windows were a physical artifact that reflected a deep belief in the value of all people.

A large financial investment company I once worked with had recently completed the construction of a beautiful new office building in the heart of the financial district of a major city. In the beginning, the people who designed the building intended to use the new structure to enhance teamwork, open communication and promote spontaneous problem solving at the place the problems occurred.

Unfortunately, when the building was complete, the senior management team decided that when customers came to visit, they wanted to communicate the message of financial success and corporate sophistication. Strict policies were created governing how the new building was and was not to be used. The result was small conference rooms far away from the workplace so that walls could be used for artwork. Strict rules were established governing what could be made visible in the office cubicles of employees.

In the end, it became clear that the company valued image and appearance far more than teamwork, communication and problem solving. The physical facility told the real story about what was most important.

DIFFUSION AND CULTURE

I read a fascinating article once about something that anthropologists often observe when studying the artifacts of ancient civilizations. The author said that archeologists and anthropologists often discover evidence that for brief periods of time the practices of one culture are imported into another culture. For example, certain aspects of the Greek culture were imported to the Roman culture. They also observed that often the adoption of these practices was short-lived. The foreign behaviors and practices appeared often to have been just a fad that was fundamentally not sustainable.

Their conclusion was that this happens when one group of people adopt the practices of another group of people without really understanding the reason why the practice was developed in the first place. They call this phenomenon "diffusion." When this happens, the practice remains superficial, perhaps even trendy, and ultimately people go back to the core of who they are and what they have learned over the long term to value the most.

In developing the Shingo Model at Utah State University, we observed companies from around the world and saw a similar diffusion occurring in modern-day organizations. Leaders would attend a conference, visit a successful company, listen to a consultant or even just read a book and try to mimic what they observed or felt to be a good thing. What they usually did was copy the program, purchase the training material or hire the "practice" leader to help them do the same thing they saw others doing. Often, the accountability for these initiatives was delegated by senior management down to middle managers in staff positions. This practice has yielded a relatively consistent outcome: lots of training, lots of projects, lots of staff, lots of meetings and some good results but also lots of turnover, lots of conflict and lots of frustration and disappointment. Ultimately, the outcomes from these initiatives were superficial and short-lived…diffusion.

Organizations that embark on these improvement "programs" routinely replace one practice for another; giving it a new name, new tools and new organizational structure. Similar to diffusion in ancient cultures, leaders of modern organizations have tried to adopt the practices of others into their culture without deep understanding, conviction or fully embracing the deeper reasons of why that practice was developed in the first place.

For leaders to build sustainable cultures of excellence, they must sincerely engage in the hard work of self-inspection, critical evaluation and personal transformation around the core beliefs that will genuinely and sustainably change the systemic beliefs and practices of the organization.

CULTURE CANNOT BE DELEGATED

The accountability for building a sustainable culture of excellence cannot be delegated downward or outward. A senior executive can solicit the support of others but the accountability for the creation and management of corporate culture must always rest squarely on the shoulders of the CEO or equivalent position.

Several years ago I was asked by the COO of an automotive industry supplier to meet with their senior management team and advise them on how they should be approaching continuous improvement. The initial meeting went great and everyone was enthusiastic about moving ahead. Naturally, I was very clear about what the leadership role had to be if they were to be successful. I also discussed what the role of the CEO specifically was in owning the overall culture of the enterprise. Although not present, they assured me that the CEO would be totally committed to this process, so we plowed in.

I then outlined the first commitment I felt it would take to really change the culture of this very old and very established company. It took a few seconds longer for a response this time but eventually everyone said yes, even though I noticed that a few wouldn't look me in the eye. I started to worry!

Shortly after getting back to my office I received an email from the newly appointed Director of Continuous Improvement informing me of his appointment and that I should work directly through him from this point forward. Now I was more than a little bit worried but we moved ahead anyway, against my better judgment.

On a phone call, I asked the new Director to schedule a two-day workshop for the senior management team. I explained that my goal was to create an experience for leaders that would help them to see the impact that their current culture was having on their current results. I then provided the list of 20 specific senior corporate and divisional leaders who must be at this session.

When the Director of Continuous Improvement finally called me back two weeks later, only five of the people on my original list of 20 were signed up. The rest of the session was to be filled by line managers and supervisors from two specific plants. Now I knew we were in trouble and I called the COO.

After an hour of conversation, I very reluctantly gave in and agreed to the process he wanted me to follow which essentially treated the plant managers as CEOs and their staff as the senior management teams. I knew this was far from ideal and that these teams would most certainly not be able to change the culture of the company from within their own relatively isolated organizations and I was right.

Only about a third of the way through our effort it became clear to all participants that what the senior management team really wanted was a project to fix the productivity and quality problems in these two plants. Every time we met, the people in my workshops demonstrated more and more frustration with trying to permanently fix problems at their level that had as their root something that was happening far above them. These were deep-seated cultural issues and fixing the culture was not something the senior management team had demonstrated a willingness to take on. The effort ultimately became unsustainable and collapsed and I learned a big lesson.

VALUES' IMPACT ON CULTURE

What leaders value the most, becomes the most powerful influence on corporate culture. Much of my work over the past 15 years has been helping leaders learn to see the behavioral impact of what they value the most. Many leaders do not take the time to consider their actions as a physical manifestation of their values. The truth is that our "values," meaning what we value, drive our behaviors. The process of making the connection between the way we act and what we value is something rarely done in business and even more rare is the process of connecting our values with the business results we are achieving.

The behaviors of the leader, being guided by what that leader has learned to value, have a profound impact on every other person in the organization. When someone or some group continues to behave in a way that seems counter to what might be best, the first place a leader should look is at his or her own behaviors. Ask yourself, "What am I doing that might be causing this behavior in others?" or "what am I doing that makes these people think that what they are doing could be OK?" Leaders lead culture every day by the demonstration of their own values as manifested in their personal behaviors.

Culture is a powerful force for good or for ill. The culture that just emerges naturally as employees observe the natural behaviors of their leaders is rarely good enough to create the conditions for global competitiveness. Architecting and purposefully designing and building a sustainable culture of excellence is deeply personal. Building culture requires leaders, managers and ultimately every frontline associate to consider carefully their own values, how those values may be influencing their personal behaviors and the behaviors of others.

One of the main reasons that changing corporate culture is so difficult, takes so long to accomplish and rarely succeeds, is because changing culture requires changing behavior. Creating a sustainable change in behavior requires a genuine and often fundamental change in what people learn to value.

> *One of the main reasons that changing corporate culture is so difficult, takes so long to accomplish and rarely succeeds, is because changing culture requires changing behavior ... and what people have learned to value.*

Changing the culture of an organization is hard work, perhaps the hardest work you will ever do. In my work with great companies I often think of the Tom Hanks line from the movie titled *A League of Their Own* where he said essentially, "*It is supposed to be hard. If it were easy everyone would be doing it.*" (We've all heard versions of the same thing.) Most certainly everyone is not doing it. Building a great culture requires vision, sustainability over the long term, self-reflection, commitment to personal improvement, humility and a genuine, deep and abiding respect for every human being.

I have observed countless organizations spend millions of dollars implementing program after program on continuous improvement only to be frustrated with their own and others' inability to change. My observation is that what leaders almost always fail to recognize is the power of the culture to keep things the way they are. Almost by definition the culture, whatever it is, is naturally designed to resist things foreign to it. That's how people learn to survive, by conforming to the culture.

Only with forces more powerful than the forces that keep it the same can cultural transformation occur. I hear so many people today talk about efforts to build continuous improvement into their culture largely by creating better programs, hiring better consultants, requiring top management participation at key events, etc. But, even knowing how hard it is to really and fundamentally change culture, more cultural improvement efforts become "programs" themselves and eventually fail for the same reasons as the continuous improvement efforts.

So, what is as powerful as the forces that protect the status quo? Just beyond survival, people want to have meaning and know that they are valued. People want to make a contribution and to know that their contribution makes a difference. The nature of people is to want to act on their own free will and to be accountable for their choices. These are traits of all human beings given to them by nature.

Successful change to a sustainable culture of excellence is best enabled when leaders acknowledge that people naturally want to find meaning, make a difference and feel valued and make these attributes foundational to their culture. For some leaders, coming to these conclusions is relatively easy, but for others, usually through years of conditioning, it is very hard. Over the years some of the most stimulating and productive conversations I have ever had with key executives have been on the topic of what is and what is not natural to people.

That people naturally want to find meaning, make a difference and feel valued is foundational to a sustainable culture of excellence.

I remember the CEO of a very large industrial company said to me when discussing the idea of empowerment; "Why Bob, we could never do that around here! That would be like turning the asylum over to the inmates." It would have been funny, and many in the room did laugh, had he not been deadly serious. His view of the employees in his company was that most were basically incompetent, dishonest, lazy and disloyal.

Hearing this almost broke my heart for the thousands of good people in that organization who got up every morning at 5:30, worked hard for 8–12 hours, often in brutal working conditions, and went home at the end of the day wondering why they did it. This was a good man who I really learned to value but one who had had many experiences over many years that almost irreparably influenced his view of the workforce.

To help organizational leaders create a sincere effort to improve their culture, I have tried to require of leaders an honest assessment of how they really view their employees. Business leaders and indeed all of us often need a small dose of reality. What we profess is often vastly different than what is actually manifested in our daily behaviors.

Before I go on, a little honesty of my own is called for. I had been teaching these ideas and principles for many years and was certain that I had them down. One day when we were testing out the questions we should be asking in an online cultural assessment we were developing, a small group of elected representatives from our staff knocked on my door and asked for permission to enter.

This cadre of reluctant folks proceeded to inform me of the almost universal feelings of disappointment that people on my team felt in my leadership. To say I was shocked would be a gross understatement! How could this be, I was the teacher?

They went on to describe how after my nearly weekly trips to client companies in many parts of the world, my habit was to come in the back door, make a beeline for my office, call my direct reports into the conference room, close the door and spend the next three or four hours in private conversation.

When asked what they thought I should do, I was told that they just wanted me to stop once in a while when I came in. They wanted me to come into their offices, ask how they were doing, check on their families and give them an opportunity to share with me what they were working on. They wanted to hear me share what I had learned from being with our customers. My smiles and warm hellos as I passed them by were far too little. Feelings that I experienced were pain, embarrassment, surprise, anger, defensiveness and eventually acceptance and gratitude. The whole cycle took about two weeks to get through.

I learned many important lessons from this experience. I wanted to believe that I valued all of the people on my team but my actions said otherwise. When I was finally able to be totally honest I had to admit that my time with the senior leadership team was really what I valued the most. My behaviors gave that away! Remember that our values drive our behaviors.

This experience forced me to think much more realistically about whether or not the things that I had come to value most were right. I knew that every one of the members of our team had great value yet my behaviors did not reflect that. What I had come to value the most, long and deep conversation with the senior management team at the expense of everyone else, was not in harmony with what I knew in my heart to be the right thing. Ouch! I will always appreciate the great employees who cared enough about their work and me to tell the truth.

Because the leader's behavior is so visible to so many people, they have the greatest impact on the culture and the one thing that cannot be delegated to someone else. The following chapters will help leaders, managers and frontline associates understand how to build a culture that will enable the potential of every employee, regardless their background or job function, and guide behaviors that lead to results for customers and every other key stakeholder.

2

Values, Behavior and Corporate Culture

*If the day-to-day work of delivering on customer promises is the **urgent**, then focusing on behaviors that yield great results is the **important**.*

The first step in improving culture is learning to see culture. When asked, everyone can describe the attributes of their organization's culture but few think about it during the normal course of conducting business. Rarely does a strategic plan or an annual plan call out specific attributes of the culture that are to be improved during the planning period.

Investments in facilities, technology, manpower, new products and new market penetration are tangible items most managers and leaders are accustomed to tracking on a spreadsheet and reporting on in weekly status updates. Changes in culture on the other hand are perceived as soft, fuzzy, difficult to manage, tough to really get your arms around and impossible to measure.

This mindset almost always results in an intense focus on results and an incidental or no focus at all on behavior or culture. Little or no focus on behavior results in a de facto culture. As stated in the opening chapter, a de facto culture rarely has the capacity to produce results sufficient to be competitive in global markets.

BEHAVIORS ARE OBSERVABLE

Behaviors are observable, describable and recordable. Culture is ultimately evidenced in behavior, which archaeologists can only speculate on. In the real world, you can see behaviors everywhere once you condition yourself to look for them. We watch the way leaders interact with each other, the way they interact with managers and frontline workers and the way they talk about the results they are accountable for, both internally and publicly.

Manager's behaviors tell associates every day what is important and what is expected. Where the manager sits relative to their teams, how much time they spend in their offices and conference rooms as opposed to out where the work is done, where they eat lunch and take breaks, how they make decisions, who gets their attention and time, who gets invited to meetings, what they do when conflict occurs in a meeting, where they park, what they measure and even how they inform people of their results are all behaviors that are noticed every day by the workforce. Leaders and managers are usually unaware of this, but their every behavior is very closely scrutinized by the workforce and become the topics of coffee breaks, lunches and after work social activities.

I took my son to work with me one day many years ago on "Take Your Child to Work Day." He told me later that he was confused and perhaps a bit disappointed when we ate lunch in the plant cafeteria with the production workers. He said to me, "Dad, I told all my friends that you were a vice president?" What a great teaching opportunity to explain that all of us were on the same team and that no one of us was better than any other. I told him that it was very important that the people see in the way I behaved that this was what I believed. Where I ate, who I sat with and even what I talked about at lunch were behaviors that demonstrated how much I valued the people.

At the time we talked about it, I remember hoping that he would see how my actions were a demonstration of my values. Twenty-five years later, this same son was running a small company in Portland, Oregon. We were having a conversation about how to resolve some issues he was experiencing with labor relations when he reminded me of our experience in the cafeteria. He told me that even all these years later, he often reflected on his observation and as a leader was trying to do the same things.

The best quote I have heard on this topic is said to be a derivative from what Ralph Waldo Emerson said in an essay titled "Social Aims" published in 1875.

"What you do speaks so loudly that I can't hear what you say." Our behaviors are out there for the world to see and are the evidence of what we believe in and who we really are.

UNDERSTANDING OUR VALUES

For several years while Executive Director of the Shingo Prize, I accepted an invitation to help teach a remedial class to incoming freshmen at Utah State University. Most of the students were in the class because they needed a boost of motivation, structure and/or direction as they commenced the rigors of higher education.

I often asked them to share with each other what their "values" were. A few had a rough idea of what I was asking but for the most part, they looked at me like I was from outer space. Rarely could they describe with any degree of clarity or specificity a set of personal beliefs that were consciously guiding the way they lived their lives. Over the semesters, I learned that I usually had to approach this question from a different direction by asking how they spent their time.

This was a much easier assignment. They often talked about their friends, their music, the video games they liked the most, how much time they spent playing them, how they spent their weekends, what time they went to bed and what time they got up in the morning, how often they called home, how much time they spent in sports and how much time they spent studying.

Having created that inventory, I then asked; "What are the things you value the most?" By now the task was becoming much easier. Notice the slight difference in the question from "What are your values?" to "What are the things that you value the most?"

Our values, the things we value the most, drive our behaviors and are almost always what govern the outcomes of our lives (or our businesses).

This became a homework assignment, hoping they would think carefully about the question. What began to become clearer to these young men and women was that the things they spent the most time on were in reality the things that they valued the most. Of those willing to admit their honest feelings about this new insight, many were somewhat disappointed to see that their values (where they spent the most time and what they valued the most) did not reflect what they had been taught, or what they suspected would lead them to a better place in life.

After sharing with each other, my young students discovered how different their individual values were from others in the class, how similar some were and how their values have changed with time. Many of them discovered that even when they said they valued the same things, upon closer inspection, their unique interpretation of the thing they valued resulted in very different behaviors.

For example, many said they valued good music, but tastes in music varied wildly. Some valued country music, others laughed at that and said they valued pop, others rock and roll and occasionally someone would say classical (even more laughs). As we discussed each of these genres of music, we always discovered that each elicited a different set of actions or behaviors. Their values were indeed driving their behaviors.

In summary, some of what we can learn from this small case study about values is:

1. It is common for people to not have ever really thought about what their values are.
2. People are routinely surprised to discover what they have come to value.
3. Our values are derived from the experiences we have had, what we have been taught or experienced and often change over time.
4. Our values have a profound influence on our choice of behavior.
5. People may say they value the same thing but personal interpretations and experiences result in a wide variety of behaviors.
6. The behaviors that values lead to always have consequences, sometimes positive and sometimes negative.

BECOMING AWARE OF OUR VALUES

Why is it important to be aware of what our values are? The answer to that question is like the *de facto culture* that just emerges while we are paying attention to getting results. Like organizational culture, a de facto life is never sufficient to be very fulfilling or contribute value to the world, or the companies we work in. If one of the keys to business improvement is to focus on helping people to improve their own behaviors, then self-awareness of values is key to self-improvement.

This is not an endorsement for T-groups or other 60s and 70s Organizational Behavior techniques. It is however, a recommendation that an important part of transforming a corporate culture is thoughtfully creating the conditions where every associate has many opportunities to evaluate their own beliefs about how they should behave and become exposed to new thinking.

Influencing personal values and behaviors is not a single event but rather the outcome of a management system that routinely presents associates with different ways to achieve great outcomes and illustrates the thinking that is required to achieve these results. The way to sustainably improve our individual approach to life and work is by learning to value the things that result in better outcomes. Our values can in fact change over time with new experiences.

Values are distinctly human traits. Corporations are inanimate things and cannot possess values. Leaders of corporations, on the other hand, do have values and often express their expectations about the values they would like individuals to possess in an organization for it to be successful. These shared, usually top-down, beliefs are often referred to as "Corporate Values."

> *Possessing values is a distinctly human trait; corporations do not possess values but leaders often express their shared expectation that employees value specific things. These are usually called "Corporate Values."*

CORPORATE VALUES

Business leaders old enough to have been working during the 80s and early 90s will remember the process many of us went through of creating company mission, vision and values statements. In 1991, I was on what we called the Board of Management for a large industrial company in Denver, Colorado. The CEO and his senior management team really wanted to restore the company to the kind of values possessed by the founding fathers in 1911. It felt to these mostly old timers that little by little and without a conscious decision, the employees no longer valued the same things. A de facto culture had replaced the culture that early corporate leaders had worked so hard to create.

An exploration of what those earlier values might have been revealed a family atmosphere where the owners knew and cared about each individual employee. I remember seeing a photograph of the corporate matriarch driving her 1918 Cole 8 coupe in an Armistice Day Parade with a large banner proclaiming 112 employees in service. The senior management team including the owners, often took time to talk to every employee; they knew their children and attended important family events like christenings, musicals or even football games.

When confronted with a business problem, leaders felt no hesitation to go directly to any employee, no matter where they worked or what level they were at. If they had expertise that could be used to help solve a problem, they became part of the solution. Owners, leaders and managers were on the floor every day talking about what was important and listening to ideas from the people about how they could make the company a better place to work.

At the top of the offices was a large auditorium called the "Roof Garden" where employees could talk with the leaders about the business and even "dance the foxtrot" during lunch hours. Several times a year the company would sponsor dances and parties for employees and their families. The company Christmas party was the event of the year where the company owners presented a gift to every child of every employee.

We all knew we could never again go back to exactly the way things used to be but we did spend a significant amount of time discussing what the early leaders believed so deeply in that caused them to behave the way they did. After careful reflection, we concluded that the founding fathers valued the following:

1. *Ownership*, including of ideas, accountabilities and results.
2. *People*, including open and trusting relationships with every employee regardless of level.
3. *Communications*, especially face-to-face, at the place where the work is being done.
4. *Recognition*, for anyone who was contributing to the wellbeing of the organization.
5. *Problem solving*, at the lowest possible level by the people closest to the problem.
6. *Innovation*, in moving forward in a way that would create differentiation and value for customers.

These values were never written down on a poster, or put on the back of the employee's badges. They were never part of an employee handbook or a performance management system, but they were deeply embedded into the everyday, unconscious behaviors of every leader and employee in the company. Leaders and managers did what they did not because it was part of a new program or associated with a tool that was being taught by HR or Quality. It was just who they were as a people. Their ideal behaviors flowed naturally from what they all valued the most. *In short, their great values drove their great behaviors and the incredible growth the company experienced!* Because each member of the leadership team genuinely valued each of these things, they became the unstated Company or Corporate Values.

In short, their great values drove their great behaviors and the incredible growth the company experienced!

When I looked around the table in our boardroom it was not hard to see that while the room was full of very competent leaders, our individual behaviors varied wildly. Of course that meant that what each leader valued and how they valued them were very, very different. We came from vastly different backgrounds, different ethnic cultures, different religions and family backgrounds. We naturally had very different values and hence very different responses to the daily issues of the global enterprise, both strategic and tactical.

Nevertheless, we dutifully went through the process of defining what we could agree on as Corporate Values that we each would commit to. Videos were made, speeches given, slogans created, posters printed, business cards updated and training conducted.

My observation, now nearly 25 years later, is that we did essentially the same thing that thousands of other companies like ours were doing all around the world. Variations, of course, included such things as perhaps defining what the behaviors of employees should be, or perhaps even putting these behavioral expectations into performance evaluations and compensation decisions.

But did it really change our deeply held and personal beliefs, our thinking and hence our natural behaviors? Did we each really genuinely embrace the intellectually calculated list of values, making each of us a new and improved version of our old, deeply habitual selves? For the most part, the answer was no!

In the years since then, I have observed in almost every one of the companies I have visited, all over the world, nearly the exact same phenomenon that we experienced in 1991. I still see the now faded posters on the walls. For most, I can find the mission, vision and values statements on their websites in the "About Us" section. Unfortunately, most of the people I have worked with, in hundreds of organizations around the world, including senior management in these companies, say that their Corporate Values are not something that are really talked about that much and certainly not something that is a compelling part of their efforts to create business improvements.

Understanding the wide variation in core values and subsequent variations in workplace behaviors is a critical insight for leaders, particularly knowing how directly the behaviors of leaders, managers and frontline associates impact business results. Because leaders are ultimately accountable for results, they must find a way to influence the beliefs and values of others without expecting everyone to give up their individuality and simply adopt the 'company line'. The goal is not to create clones where everyone thinks and acts the same, but rather allowing individuals the freedom to express their unique gifts and also help them to align their own beliefs with the values of the organization.

Influencing beliefs cannot be done through policy, email, newsletters, speeches or even financial incentives. Changing personal beliefs and behavior can only be accomplished through a sustained focus on

1. Education
2. Coaching
3. Engagement
4. Personal experiences
5. Observing and discussing the cause and effect relationship between results and behaviors

OUR VALUES COME FROM OUR EXPERIENCES

In some parts of the world, people still live relatively simple lives where members of a community may all attend the same church, go to the same public schools, have the same teachers, live in the same neighborhoods and even shop in the same stores. In these conditions it would be likely for the people in that community to share very common values. In 1911 when the company I mentioned above was in its formative years, the community they started in was much smaller and relatively homogenous, producing people with very similar values; not so today.

I am often asked why it seems to be so much easier for companies in parts of Mexico to create such great cultures. In the last 20 years I have spent a great deal of time getting to know many of the wonderful people working in many Mexican companies. I have been to their homes and attended family and community events.

My observation is that the Mexican culture is relatively consistent by many other Western European and US standards. Most people belong to the same religion, families are generally very strong and for the most part, people are warm, personable and respectful. People are generally very happy to be working and are eager to learn.

These are generalizations for sure, but they are my experiences. By hiring mostly employees who possess these shared values, many Mexican leaders are able to more easily align people's thinking and values in a way that leads to a positive and sustainable culture of excellence.

In the world where most of us live, our companies are filled with people from wildly diverse backgrounds. I know of a company in Salt Lake City that has employees from over 80 different countries. Political divides are wide and getting wider. The Internet and social media have a powerful influence on people's thinking and hence what they come to value. Multinational corporations mix employees from entirely different backgrounds in an effort to share best practices and bring divisions of the same company closer together.

These are the people who come to work in our companies. They think differently, manage differently, follow differently, problem solve differently, learn differently and communicate differently. Having such a broad spectrum of people in a single organization is more common than not. Weaving this diversity into a purposefully architected culture is hard work and requires great skill. The key word in the above statement is "purposefully." This means leaders must decide what it is that they want to align beliefs around and what behaviors are most likely to create the kind of results they are accountable to deliver.

ALIGNING INDIVIDUAL VALUES

The behaviors of frontline associates, meaning all of people who do the direct work of providing goods and/or services for customers, also are physical manifestations of their values. Their behaviors speak to what they have learned to value in life, what is most important to them and what they believe to be the best way to get along in the workplace. Examples of observable behaviors include

- What they do when they see something that just "doesn't feel right"
- How they approach personal development
- What they do with ideas for improvement
- How they interact with other associates and their managers

Some of these behaviors are observable just by looking but others may require many long conversations. Observing behavior is step number one, understanding what is causing or driving the behavior is a significant leadership challenge and the key to changing culture. Some behaviors may only be understood after investing in a relationship of trust.

Observing behavior is the first step; understanding what is driving the behavior is the key to changing culture.

FOCUS ON BEHAVIORS

In many places where I have worked, use of the word "behavior" seems inappropriate and out of place in the context of a business discussion. "Behavior" is often used in the context of children or teenagers. Frequently it is considered in relation to a person's bad behaviors. For others it is just something that you don't discuss at work, or if you do it is done in Human Resources or by internal Organizational Behavior specialists.

Tangible results are the reason we come to work and discussing behaviors relative to work, unless they are particularly bad behaviors, is often considered soft, too complicated, personal and very often, uncomfortable. If the day-to-day, hour-to-hour, minute-to-minute work of delivering on customer promises is what Stephen Covey called the *urgent* work of the business, then focusing on behaviors that yield great results is the *important.* For most of us, the urgent almost always trumps the important. "Highly effective people", as Dr. Covey taught, are able to put first things first (Covey 1989). Creating behaviors that yield a high performing culture comes first followed closely by a focus on the required results.

I often ask managers, "On a scale of one to ten, where do your leaders tend to focus their time and attention: more on results or more on behaviors?" Without exception, people everywhere say that their leaders are focused primarily on results, most often followed by a few nervous jokes and sideward glances to make sure everyone else said the same thing.

If the day-to-day work of delivering on customer promises is the **urgent***, then focusing on behaviors that yield great results is the* **important***.*

It is no surprise that the higher you get to the top of an organization, the more attention you must give to obtaining results; someone has to! Board meetings rarely focus on the behaviors of people, that is, until a key leader's behavior presents a clear and present danger to the results they expect to see, then it becomes a crisis.

Most of us tend to look past the behaviors of others until they become so bad or egregious that they can no longer be overlooked. We need only look as far as many of our political leaders to see evidence of this.

In the workplace performance evaluations often focus on the degree to which an employee achieves specified performance objectives set at the beginning of a planning period. Conversations about behavior, when they do occur, typically focus on a person's strengths and weaknesses rather than on the day-to-day choices about how to act in the face of day-to-day events. When specific ideal behaviors are not described, expected, observed, measured, evaluated and improved, the behaviors that just happen on their own are the de facto behaviors.

I know of many companies, even consulting firms, that resist conversations about values. Their argument is that conversations about values have no place in the context of work. They prefer to talk about behaviors as though all that is required is to describe for employees the required behaviors and then communicate performance expectations.

My experience, however, is that discussions of values cannot be avoided when trying to change organizational culture. Individual values profoundly influence individual behaviors and culture is in fact the sum of those behaviors. Efforts to change culture must of necessity include a change in what people believe and value. Efforts to change culture without acknowledging

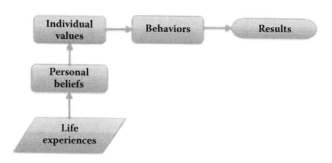

FIGURE 2.1
Relationship between experiences and results.

and focusing on values and behaviors, become programs or a series of projects. When the program ends most people simply return to what they believe is in their best interest, or what they have learned over time to value the most.

> *Efforts to change culture without acknowledging and focusing on values and behaviors, become programs or just a series of projects.*

Almost every organization I have ever worked with or know of has proven, usually repeatedly, that organizational improvement efforts that do not focus on changing individual values and behaviors are fundamentally unsustainable.

The illustration, Figure 2.1, summarizes the relationship between our experiences, our beliefs, our values, our behaviors and our results.

Any effort to fundamentally and sustainably improve results cannot avoid the difficult work of changing what people believe as the right way to behave.

SUSTAINABLE CULTURES OF ENTERPRISE EXCELLENCE

Understanding where behaviors come from and their impact on results prepares us to talk about cultures and cultures of excellence specifically. If leaders are to create great results they must also be responsible for creating a culture that is capable of delivering great results over the long term. This is what I refer to as a "sustainable culture of enterprise excellence." Because every leader's ultimate goal should be to create a sustainable culture of enterprise excellence, let's break down the keywords: sustainable, culture, enterprise, and excellence.

1. **Sustainable** means ideal results are created and delivered in a way that is capable of being repeated over and over for the long term.
2. **Culture** is observed in the learned and demonstrated behavioral patterns of people in an organization.
3. **Enterprise** is the entire scope of an organization; from top to bottom and from side to side.
4. **Excellence** is the creation of results that are recognized by customers as maximizing the creation of value to them and provides fair value for all other stakeholders.

Cultures do not change quickly. What people come to value happens a little bit at a time over a very long time. It is not practical to expect values and behaviors to change just because a senior management team provided a new list of what the company states as the values of its employees. Organizational leaders should ask, "What will it really take for people to not only understand the company values, but also deeply believe them to be correct and then align their unconscious daily behaviors with those values?"

Individual values can change over time given a new set of experiences and insight, but because values are so deeply personal, leaders must respect individuality and at the same time begin to align many unique points of view into a homogenous network of ideal behaviors that maximize customer value creation. In the next chapter we will begin to explore how this may be done.

This work of influencing the behaviors of hundreds if not thousands of associates may be the most difficult work that any leader will ever engage in. I will repeat; a failure to purposefully focus on behaviors will result in a "de facto" culture that will never have the capacity to compete in an increasingly competent and global economy.

Influencing the behaviors of all associates may be the most difficult work that any leader will ever engage in.

So, the next emerging questions for great leaders are:

1. Which behaviors are most ideal?
2. What must people believe in order for those ideal behaviors to become natural to them?
3. How do I shape my employees' beliefs and values to help them, on their own, want to behave in an ideal way?"

The answer to these questions will be explored in coming chapters.

3

Principles and Foundational Truths

Because values govern behaviors and principles govern consequences, value principles.

Stephen Covey

For years I used the words "values" and "principles" interchangeably and have noticed that most people do the same thing. They are not! This chapter will focus on describing in detail the many intricacies of what a principle is. As the chapter closes I will try to summarize the differences between values and principles and explain why is it critical for leaders to know the difference.

From the previous chapter you recall that a value is a deeply held belief about what is important to each person. What we value the most has the greatest impact on our daily choice of behaviors. Values are influenced by our unique experiences and are likely to change over time as we mature and experience different things in life. Stephen Covey once told me that he believed that the best way to improve recidivism in prisons is to change what the inmates' value in their lives. When new values replace old ones, individual behaviors begin to change and become sustainable over the long term.

This was the relationship we described in the previous chapter illustrating how our experiences influence our beliefs, which inform our values. Our values are what guide our behaviors, which of course govern the outcomes of our life. In business terms we would say our behaviors determine to a large degree the results we are able to contribute to the organization.

Because every single person comes to work every day with a unique set of experiences, their own values and their unique behavioral response to every work situation, it begs the question, "What makes one value better than another value?" An even more complex variant on the question is, "What makes the way one person values something any better than the way someone else may value the same thing?" The only possible answer has to be in the quality of the behavior and outcome that the value engenders.

For example, a felon may value teamwork, loyalty and innovation in the way they conduct a burglary, but a police officer may also value teamwork, loyalty and innovation in the way they pursue and capture the criminal. The officer and the felon claim the same values, but they also demonstrate entirely different behaviors and outcomes. It is in this difference that we begin to discover the meaning of a principle and how a principle is different than a value.

Teamwork, loyalty and innovation are values. They differ in meaning based on the experience of each unique individual. Their meaning and application change over time and our diverse interpretation of them drives our various behaviors. What then makes the difference between the felon and the policeman both possessing the same values?

FRAMEWORK FOR UNDERSTANDING PRINCIPLES

Because a discussion of principles is not a typical business conversation, the following illustration (Figure 3.1) may be helpful in framing the discussion of a principle. This model will be referenced throughout the chapter.

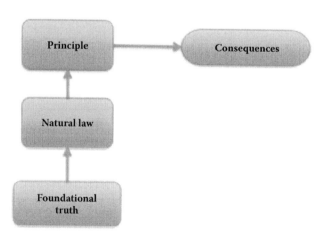

FIGURE 3.1
Framework for a principle.

THE VOICE OF A PRINCIPLE

A principle differs from a value in that it is not subject to personal interpretation; it is a statement of fact that expresses a natural law. Natural laws exist in nature not in the mind or personal opinion of individuals. Laws of nature have at their root some foundational truth. A foundational truth is something that has always been, is now and will always be the way things are. The fixed nature of a foundational truth is the reason a natural law stays the same over time and gives efficacy to a principle. This is a complex statement that will become much clearer as we advance through the chapter.

> *The fixed nature of a foundational truth is the reason a natural law stays the same over time and gives efficacy to a principle.*

A principle is usually a statement of action that describes the natural law and when followed, governs an outcome. Principles are usually expressed in a way that describes a cause and effect. If you do this, you get that. Principles describe laws of nature that are irrefutable. Men and women do not create principles, they only discover them. Man-made laws attempt to mimic laws of nature by describing actions that should be taken in a society. If you follow the law, everything will be fine, but if you do not, the law usually describes some negative consequence. The difference is that societal laws are man-made; they change over time and their validity is constantly being challenged for one reason or another. In this respect natural laws are much different than man-made laws.

Sir Isaac Newton noticed that if you drop an apple it always falls downward. I notice that if I drop my cell phone it will always fall onto the floor. It is certain and predictable. When an object heavier than air is dropped, it always falls downward. This statement of action that describes a cause and effect is an example of a natural law. It simply states the relationship between the behavior (letting go of the object having mass) and the consequence (the object falls downward). It is a law of nature that exists; it just does.

A natural law is true everywhere, it has always been true and will be true as long as we can conceive. A foundational truth is the core of the law and what makes it true, universal and timeless. The foundational truth is what makes natural law certain and predictable. It is what gives efficacy and speaks to the principle. In the case of gravity, the foundational truth is that "there is a natural force that attracts any body toward the center of the earth, or toward any other physical body having mass." Because this is true, if you release any object having mass, it will always fall downward and toward the center of the earth. This is the natural law. It doesn't matter if I am in England, China or Peru; it doesn't matter which side of the equator I am on or in which millennia I might have dropped it; the law always applies and governs the same outcome. Any tool or weapon ever created that is based on this natural law of gravity will work today exactly as it did eons ago.

Scientists study these natural laws and foundational truths so that they better understand what it is that makes them universal, timeless and predictable. The more they understand, the better able they are to create powerful tools or instruments that solve complex problems and do valuable work.

Because principles are the actionable manifestation of a natural law, for purposes of simplification, from this point forward in the work, I will use the terms interchangeably.

PRINCIPLES GOVERN CONSEQUENCES (OUTCOMES)

In order for a principle to govern an outcome, or in the language of business, a result, a principle must be a statement of action. A principle states that when we do something (the action), something will happen (the consequence or the result). A principle must have a subject and a predicate, or a noun and a verb. Together the statement forms a principle. The outcome of a principle is a consequence of the action.

Because the principle is based on a foundational truth and describes an action that has a predictable outcome, understanding the principle enables me to make good decisions about how I should act. Over time and by carefully observing the consequence of my actions, influenced by my values, what I learn to value becomes strongly influenced by my understanding of principles. Stephen Covey taught that because values govern behaviors but principles govern consequences, what we should learn to value are principles.

Because values govern behaviors and principles govern consequences, value principles.

Stephen R. Covey

I was helping a great company once refresh their stated corporate values based on their new understanding of principles when we discovered that the values they professed and how they intended that those values manifest themselves were indeed already based on principles. All we had to do was make the connection and when talking about the values reference the associated principle as a way of helping others understand why they value what they do. In the beginning it felt like it might be a bit of a burden and complication but within a few months everyone had learned the new language and it became completely natural. Understanding the principles helped them to develop many new and innovative ways to reinforce the applicable principles and illustrate for people how the principles gave voice to and informed their values and behaviors.

Principles govern both positive and negative consequences. If a person chooses to ignore the principle we call gravity, then by default, that person is also choosing to accept the outcomes. If a purchasing manager chooses to ignore the rising cost of raw materials, then they must be prepared to accept the associated increase in product cost that results from them. Natural laws cannot be ignored without experiencing some version of the consequences. Simply saying that I do not believe that material costs will rise does not negate the consequences on product cost when they do and you are unprepared for them.

Every behavior has a consequence, either positive or negative. If it is based on a principle, the consequence will almost always be positive; if the behavior disregards a principle, the consequence will almost always be negative. We cannot avoid the consequences of our actions; they are as certain as ignoring the physical law or principle we call gravity. There is always a principle that either intentionally we have acted on or inadvertently ignored.

If we place short-term profits ahead of quality we will eventually reap the consequence that the loss of confidence by our customers will have. This outcome is based on a principle we call *create value for customers*. If we do not engage our employees in improving the processes they are responsible for, we will reap the consequence of their lack of ownership and personal accountability. This is based on the principle we call *respect for every individual*. If we make decisions that affect one area without considering the implications for others both upstream and down, we will reap the unintended and unplanned negative consequences of our actions on others. This consequence is based on disregarding the principle of *thinking systemically*.

If we do not engage our employees in improving the processes they are responsible for, we will reap the consequence of their lack of ownership and personal accountability.

Wise leaders learn to think about the consequences of their actions before acting. Principles are a powerful lens through which great behavioral choices can be made. By purposefully and carefully listening to the voice of principles before a decision is made, leaders can learn to better evaluate the likely consequence of their actions before acting. The better we are at hearing the voice of principles, the more competent we become at predicting the outcomes we will almost certainly experience.

By purposefully and carefully listening to the voice of principles before a decision is made, leaders can learn to better evaluate the likely consequence of their actions before acting.

Early on in the process of building an organizational culture based on principles it is very difficult to remember to think about the principles but with time, support and great management systems, it can become instinctive to everyone. When this happens others are likely to describe you and your organization as being *highly principled*.

CATEGORIES OF PRINCIPLES

Principles may be organized or categorized into any number of headings. Useful categories of principles that serve only as examples might include:

1. Principles that govern the physical world around us including the law of gravity or the reaction of different chemicals when combined or the forces that keep the universe in balance
2. Principles that govern successful relationships and human interactions, such as many of Dr. Covey's *Seven Habits*
3. Principles that relate to human nature such as the need for belonging
4. Principles that relate to man's relationship with Deity, such as faith
5. Principles that govern the execution of a successful business enterprise

Principles that govern the execution of a successful business enterprise will be the particular focus of this work but as you will discover as you explore these principles more deeply, many principles may accurately be placed under multiple headings.

PRINCIPLES ARE TIMELESS

Principles do not change over time. If I stepped off of a building 100 years ago or a thousand years ago or at the beginning of a planning period or at the end of a five-year plan, the outcome can be counted on to be the same. If I decide to invest in the education and development of my employees, I can be certain that the benefits of making this investment will be valuable long after the cost has been fully depreciated. This happens because my decision to invest in people is based on a principle. A choice to invest in people has always been a good choice. There has never been a time when ignoring the potential of people to learn was a good decision, nor will there ever be such a time.

What I choose to train employees in, however, may be based entirely on the personal values of an individual leader or manager. One manager may value the latest technology for organizing and retrieving information but another manager may place greater value in his or her employees being skilled in managing the resolution of conflicts in the workplace. Both managers are committed to the development of people (the principle) but the individual approach is based on the values of the unique manager. The specific development opportunities provided to employees will change over time (based on values) but the fact that the people need and value their personal development will remain constant.

If I base a product strategy on the collective values of a particular market segment, I must be prepared for my products to become obsolete when current events and competitor's products fundamentally change the things that customers value. No place is this more evident than in technology related industries. What customers value at the moment changes with time, often a short time. That their purchasing decision is based on the degree to which they believe I have created greater value for them than anyone else is based on a principle and will always be true, *create value for customers*. How I organize my business must provide at least equal and perhaps even greater focus on creating an environment that ensures long term responsiveness to changing values as it does to providing for today's current demand.

> *How I organize my business must provide at least equal and perhaps even greater focus on creating a culture that ensures long term responsiveness to changing values as it does to providing for today's current demand.*

Values change over time while principles are timeless. Basing the culture of an organization on the voice of principles rather than values will result in the ability to provide solutions to problems and respond to changing values in a way that provides much greater sustainability over the long term.

PRINCIPLES ARE SELF-EVIDENT

Dr. Stephen Covey in his book, *Seven Habits of Highly Effective People*, taught that principles are inarguable because they are self-evident (Covey 1989). What part of business is inarguable? It certainly isn't the product or service that we provide or our understanding of the market or customer demand. It is not our understanding of our competitors or the best strategy to respond to a new opportunity. The number or kind of employees we might hire that will have the greatest impact is not self-evident nor is who should get promoted versus who should be let go. None of these decisions are self-evident and are therefore arguable.

Values and individual interpretations of a value are by definition personal and variable and hence are not self-evident. It is impossible to build the foundation of a culture that is to be ideal and sustainable over the long term on anything that is individually interpretable, variable, changeable with time and arguable. Culture must be based on principles that are universal, timeless and inarguable because they are self-evident; basing culture on anything else is by definition short-term. Self-evident means that when I understand the principles well enough, I see for myself that it is irrefutable.

> *Culture must be based on principles that are universal, timeless and inarguable because they are self-evident; basing culture on anything else is by definition short-term.*

Some principles are easier to understand than others. Some are instantly self-evident; others may require weeks, months or perhaps even years to understand well enough for them to become self-evident.

I worked with a research organization once that was trying to implement a program of continuous improvement. Many very bright people struggled to understand the connections between values, behaviors, principles and results. To help them through this, we discussed the nature of the science they were developing right in their own facilities. We talked about why they did what they did, and the natural laws they were learning from it. We then discussed what good might happen in the world by understanding these laws and the foundational truths they were based on.

Most of the natural laws they were researching only became self-evident after many years of research, but once it was understood it seemed simple and they wondered why they hadn't seen it all along. The consequences of the principles they discovered were immense for all of humanity.

What my students came to see was that just like the principles related to physics, many other kinds of natural laws can only be understood by observing the outcomes or effects that the law or principle is governing. The more that people understand the underlying principles that govern the outcomes, the more self-evident the principle becomes and the more powerful a person becomes by purposefully acting in harmony with the principle.

AN EXAMPLE OF A PRINCIPLE OF ENTERPRISE EXCELLENCE

Even though it will be discussed in great detail in a later chapter, I will use one of the principles of Enterprise Excellence as an example. The principle is *"Respect Every Individual."* Respect is the subject. In this case respect is also a verb, the action and something that you do. "Every Individual" is the predicate. Together they describe a principle, a statement of action that governs an outcome. When you demonstrate respect for every individual you can predict what the outcome will be.

The outcomes associated with demonstrating respect for every individual have always existed. That we should demonstrate respect for every individual was true a thousand years ago; it is true now and it will be true a thousand years from now. It most certainly will be true at the end of the planning cycle for our organizations.

Demonstrating *Respect for Every Individual* applies to every culture in any part of the world. Many cultures have emerged based on fear, control, power or some other individual value. Often these values of a leader may even be deeply ingrained in a culture, but the principle remains true. People will always respond positively when treated with respect. Some may be suspicious or perhaps even frightened at first, but when they discover that your respect is genuine, they will respond in a positive manner and become more engaged and committed to your effort.

I was working in an Asian country a few years ago. People told me that these ideas would not work in that country because they had a culture where the government controlled virtually every aspect of the business. People were told exactly what to do and every detail about how it was to be done. Failure to comply precisely to stated policies had severe consequences. This system of management had been deeply ingrained into all aspects of work and in every industry.

What I actually experienced however, after working in their country for several years, were people who were eager to learn, hungry to participate and capable far beyond what they had previously been allowed to contribute. I observed that government owned and operated businesses stifled the natural inclinations of people, but privately owned and operated businesses using the same workforce were entirely different. This insight contributed to my curiosity about what it is inside of us that connects so naturally with principles, even when the culture around us may be doing everything possible to hold it back.

This topic deserves deep personal reflection. Those who believe in some higher power, as I do, may attribute this to a divine spark placed in the hearts of all men and women. This spark is what gives us our nature and when we hear a principle or a law of nature, we feel its rightness even more powerfully than we hear it in our minds. I will share my observations and learning related to this very interesting hypothesis in the following chapter.

TESTING FOR A PRINCIPLE

I have been teaching principles to corporate executives for over ten years. As we discuss each principle, I ask them to apply the following test.

1. Does it govern outcomes?
2. Is it universal?
3. Is it timeless?
4. Is it inarguable because it is self-evident?

When discussing principles, I often do it by challenging people to find something about the principles that they fundamentally disagree with, something that might refute the argument that the principle is in fact universal, timeless and inarguable. Invariably, after sometimes heated but always enlightening debate, we come to agree that indeed the concept is in fact a principle. Some are easier to defend than others and some principles seem to be more profoundly impactful than others. Nevertheless, if they meet the four criteria above, they are most likely principles.

About ten years ago while teaching a group of very, very intelligent senior level executives in a very successful company, one of them, who happened to have a PhD in philosophy, asked me the question, "So Bob, what is it specifically that makes these statements universal and timeless? How do they govern outcomes?" Up until that point I was essentially asking them to "trust me." I stared at him for a few seconds; we had a very long and very public conversation but in the end I was not very satisfied that I knew how to answer his questions and that for me to be credible I had to know the answers.

The reason why we are well served to keep drilling deeper in our understanding of principles is because the more deeply we understand the principle, the better able we are to predict the outcomes that it governs and make better choices about how to act and lead. That being the case, the question of my philosopher friend is entirely appropriate to answer.

I knew that principles were natural laws, things that we didn't invent and I knew that they have always existed. I knew that if I acted in a way that was congruent with the principle, I could predict a certain outcome. The principle described the statement of action that governed the outcome. But *why* was this so and *why* has it always been so?

WHY SHOULD WE RESPECT EVERY INDIVIDUAL?

To answer that question, I will again draw forward from Chapter 6 using the principle of *Respect Every Individual*. We should feel and demonstrate respect not only for people who are easy to respect, but also for those who are different than us, not just when they are doing well but also when they may be struggling. Behaviors that are consistent with the principle of respect for every person, lead to consistent and ideal outcomes. The principle is a statement of action that has a predictable cause and effect relationship. Why does treating someone with respect predictably yield a positive outcome? The answer to this question is crucial and will lead to a deeper understanding of other principles of enterprise excellence.

APPLYING THE "5 WHYS"

In business I was taught to apply a tool called the *5 Whys* in searching for the root cause to a problem. Asking *why* five times usually reveals more and more insight to the problem until eventually, usually by the time you ask it five times, you will have uncovered the root of the problem or question.

Using this same approach to understanding a principle helps to reach a deeper understanding of the *why* behind the principle, or the reason why the principle-based action yields a consistent and predictable result, and always has.

Using our example, one might ask, as I did...

1st Why: Why should we treat every person with respect?
A: "Because they will be more loyal and committed to the purposes of the organization they are a part of."

Could this really be the root? Do I treat someone with respect just so I can get more out of him or her? Treating someone in a certain way so that I can get something out of them is deceitful and disrespectful. Respect does not have a pre-condition. I soon concluded that this might be a true statement, but it is an effect not a cause and "sits on the other side of the principle," meaning it is an outcome of the principle but not a reason for why I should respect every individual. The reason why sits below the principle and this answer sat above the principle. Let's keep going.

2nd Why: Why do people feel more loyal and committed when they feel respected?

A: "Because people want to be valued and genuine respect leads to behaviors that demonstrate a belief in the value of a person."

Could this be the root cause for the efficacy of the principle? I felt like we were getting closer. Studies show that what people want most out of their work experience is to know that they are making a difference and that their contribution is valued and respected. This felt better because at least now it wasn't about me; it was about the other person. It felt more respectful. Even though this answer was on the correct side of the principle, I wondered if the ultimate answer could be even further below; so we asked again.

3rd Why: Why do people want to feel valued?
A: "Because they are not objects; they are human beings. People are not tools, equipment or facilities. People are living things and as such, their value is innate and each one is inherently worthy of respect."

Sadly, in many organizations inanimate objects such as buildings, machines, computers etc. are categorized on the books and often in the minds of senior leaders, as "assets." We invest in them for their ability to improve results. Conversely, we often categorize people as "liabilities," things that add cost and should be minimized to the degree possible. This mindset is fundamentally one of disrespect for the "human being" in favor of the "thing." So now I knew two reasons why I should treat every person with respect: one, because they are human beings with value, and two, that inside of all people lies the desire to be of value and to be recognized as having value. Now we were getting somewhere, but was that the end? One more *why* did the trick.

4th Why: Why should human beings be valued differently than physical assets?
A: "Because unlike machines, buildings and other physical assets, people don't depreciate over time."

People have an almost infinite potential to learn, grow, improve and add greater and greater levels of value to the organization. When we see a person, we should see them not just for who they are now, but also for what they may become. This is their untapped potential. When I hire someone,

I hire that person not just for their current abilities but also for their ability to learn, grow and contribute far greater things in the future. Enabling this growth then becomes a leadership role.

I know of a unique organization that places great value in seniority. By that I mean that they have great respect for those with grey hair and experience. Rather than putting them to pasture, more mature individuals are given responsibilities to counsel, mentor, coach and advise younger, less experienced individuals. This mindset and system of leadership pays great dividends to both the older and the younger people in the organization. Growth for both groups is accelerated and continued long past the time when others might be sitting in front of a television just passing the time away and depreciating in value.

THE ROOT OF THE PRINCIPLE

After just four why's we have come to a much deeper understanding of the principle of *Respect Every Individual*. We have essentially answered my friend's question. What is it about this principle that makes it universal, timeless and inarguable? It is the fact that individuals or people are human beings, innately worthy of respect and possessing powerful and untapped potential to grow. Because this is true, therefore I respect all of them. Some might ask, "Really, all of them?" I've thought about this challenge for a very long time and can think of no one unworthy of my/our respect.

This does not mean by any stretch that I approve of all of their behaviors or what they have or haven't done with their lives. But, they are still human beings with innate value and untapped potential. For every situation that has been argued against respecting someone, a hundred stories can be told about individuals in the same situation that turned their lives around and became something far better.

I have a very close friend who from birth has possessed a significant mental disability. Many have written him off as having little or no value. He almost never leaves his home, does almost no work and often places a burden on others who must care for him. Yet, almost everyone who takes the time to interact with him for even a few minutes leaves the encounter uplifted and edified. Even with many permanent disabilities, my friend consistently adds value to society. He is a human being, has innate value, untapped potential and is worthy of respect. This can be said for anyone.

These conclusions have always been true. They are true now and will be true eons into the future. Because this is so, I call it a foundational truth. This foundational truth enables the principle of *Respect for Every Individual* to in fact be a natural law, consistently and predictably governing certain outcomes. The principle is built on a foundational truth that is immutable.

This then is why we should *Respect Every Individual.* This is why we can predict that the outcome of treating a person in this way will be increased loyalty, less turnover, greater creativity and innovation, higher levels of participation and a desire to contribute not just their hands but also their heads and their hearts. It is impossible to quantify the value of this level of commitment, but when you treat people with respect, these outcomes are almost always predictable.

In my experience one of the greatest outcomes of treating every individual with respect is the incredible feeling of satisfaction that comes from seeing people flourish as a consequence of the respect shown towards them. Naturally, not all people respond the same, but the probability of change for the better is much greater in a culture of respect. That people respond positively to being respected and the associated feelings of satisfaction for the person doing the respecting has always been true, it is true now and will be true long into the future. It is one of the principles that you can build a culture on.

This foundational truth is really the part that is most inarguable. The principle that flows from it is the statement of action about what you do because you understand the foundational truth. In the example provided, because I know that every human being has intrinsic value and untapped potential, therefore I respect every individual. Conversely, the reason why I respect every individual is because I know that they are human beings, with innate value and untapped potential. The foundational truth is the *why* below the principle. The act of demonstrating respect yields a predictable outcome because the action is based on a foundational truth.

PEOPLE AND FOUNDATIONAL TRUTHS

For every principle, there is a foundational truth or perhaps more than one. In coming chapters we will explore foundational truths associated with other principles. As we spent the better part of a year exploring each of the principles of Enterprise Excellence, we noticed that the truths that began to become more and more clear to us all had to do with people.

At the root of each principle we found something that had to do with what is true about people: what motivates them, what enables them or what is in their nature. This was a particularly surprising insight because we were talking about principles that had to do with the execution of business strategy. I knew that people were an important component of any organization but I never supposed that achieving excellent and sustainable results was so deeply connected to what was inside of every individual in the organization.

Since gaining these insights some have softened the concept by calling these statements fundamental "beliefs" or concepts. By doing this, I believe a significant part of the argument is lost for the voice of the principle. Principles are based on natural laws that have always existed. Values are personal beliefs. Our goal is to understand the universal principles, not individual values or beliefs, and to understand them with sufficient depth and conviction that our actions become predictable throughout the entire planning horizon.

If an enterprise is to invest the time and emotional commitment to embed something into the culture, they must be certain that what they are doing is not just someone's belief that may or may not turn out to be true at some point during the life of the enterprise. Specific tactics developed to execute the business plan may reasonably be based on beliefs grounded in trends or current preferences, but the way they are implemented must be grounded in universal and timeless principles.

A sustainable culture of excellence must be built on a sure foundation of fact rather than hoped for beliefs that things might possibly turn out a certain way. It is because a principle is based on truths rather than beliefs that it becomes universal, timeless, inarguable and predictable.

Every leader should take the time to study not only the principles but also the foundational truths they are based on. This process is not for the faint of heart and is best done over time with colleagues who will push back with lots of why's. When you ask the *why* question, ask yourself, "Which side of the principle am I talking about? Am I on the effect side of the principle or am I on the cause side, am I above or below the principle?"

Keep asking why, not only to yourself but also to your colleagues. I am certain that we have only just begun to understand all of the foundational truths below each of the ten principles of enterprise excellence.

Again; the more deeply a person understands a principle, the more capable they are of making good choices about how to behave in any situation. Leaders, managers and frontline associates all become far more able to wisely consider the consequences of their behaviors when they understand and think carefully about foundational truths and the principles that govern the outcomes we desire to achieve.

The more deeply a person understands a principle, the more capable they are of making good choices about how to behave in any situation.

Without listening carefully to the voice of principles, we are simply acting on a tactical level. By considering all applicable principles in every decision, we are being strategic.

Understanding, then acting on our understanding brings conviction. Conviction changes values. Changed values result in changed behavior. Changed behaviors result in a changed culture, and *create a sustainable culture of enterprise excellence...based on principles.*

By considering all applicable principles in every decision, we are being strategic.

IDEAL BEHAVIOR

As leaders become more aware of principles and the foundational truths that sit below them, an interesting phenomenon occurs: their standard of excellence begins to go up. In many cases expectations go dramatically up. In performing organizational assessments over the years, I have observed the level of behavioral and performance expectations of its leaders is one of the telltale leadership behaviors indicating the degree to which they are attuned with principles.

As leaders become more aware of principles and the foundational truths that sit below them, an interesting phenomenon occurs: their standard of excellence begins to go up.

I worked for a CEO once who I considered by any standard to be a deeply principled person. I also found him to be one of the most demanding people I have ever worked for. His expectations of both behaviors and results were driven by his deep commitment to a few key principles that governed his life. He expected everyone in his organization to be governed by the same things and deliver at the level that the voice of the principles predicated.

It is interesting that leaders recognize bad behavior when they see it and they can usually describe what good behavior looks like, but describing "ideal" behavior is often very difficult and requires a very different lens than the one we most often see the world through. When thinking about business outcomes, most of us have had plenty of practice describing ideal work, ideal project management, ideal engineering or ideal planning, but when thinking of behaviors, few have had the opportunity or coaching to plan for and recognize the ideal behaviors that have the greatest potential to create ideal and sustainable business results.

What is ideal to one person may be average to another. I see this all of the time. Because we ultimately want to measure culture, we must have some kind of a standard to which we can compare the behavior that we are seeing. This standard cannot be the opinion of a person and cannot be based on personal values, since values differ by person and change over time. This challenge of describing and measuring behavior or culture is only resolved by understanding principles.

When it comes to behavior, an annual performance review, the personal expectations of individual managers or posted guidelines from Human Resources rarely provide sufficient detail. Rarely does an organization have a system or the resources available to help people understand what makes behavior ideal and what they must believe to make these behaviors a natural part of their daily work. This bears repeating. For ideal behaviors to become a natural part of daily work, people must believe deeply in and value the core ideas or principles that lead to those behaviors.

> *For ideal behaviors to become a natural part of daily work, people must believe deeply in and value the core ideas or principles that lead to those behaviors.*

IDEAL RESULTS REQUIRE IDEAL BEHAVIOR

The more that leaders and managers talk about behaviors, the more visible they become and they learn to see behaviors for their ability to impact the creation of ideal results. Average to good results can generally be mustered with average, everyday, normal behavior. Very good results require very good behaviors but *ideal results require ideal behaviors.* This insight requires a deeper examination of what makes a result ideal and what makes a behavior ideal.

> *Average to good results can generally be mustered with average, everyday, normal behavior. Very good results require very good behaviors but ideal results require ideal behaviors.*

Ideal results are those that clearly and sustainably maximize value for customers. Ultimately ideal results should be defined within the context of new product launches, pricing that is seen as a good value, short order to cash cycle times or perhaps growth of the business or growth in a new market segment. Ideal results metrics may also be found in Volatile Organic Compounds (VOC's) emitted, total energy consumed, surgeries performed successfully, lives saved, correct packages delivered, loans serviced, claims processed or customer services rendered. Ideal results are those results that customers, those for whom the organization exists, will happily continue to pay for. Ideal results are results that are sustainable over the long term. They are what should be clearly articulated in the strategic and annual plans for the business. They are also usually lagging indicators. By definition, a result is usually a measurement of how well something worked. Focusing on the lagging indicator without equal or greater attention to what is causing those outcomes is like treating the symptom for a problem without ever getting to its root cause.

Ideal behaviors are one of the key drivers in achieving ideal results; in fact, ideal results require ideal behavior. A good strategic plan for example must not only direct specific capital investments required to achieve an ideal result, but must also identify the ideal behaviors required to achieve and sustain those results over the long term.

The identification of what an ideal behavior is can only be made through the voice of a principle. At every juncture a leader and indeed the entire leadership team should be asking, "What must our behaviors be and what must the behaviors of others be if we are to be successful at this thing?" To answer that question thoroughly they must also ask, "What are the principles that govern the success of this initiative and how will hearing the voice of that principle enable our success?"

PRINCIPLES AND BUREAUCRACY

In the absence of principles, people create bureaucracy. This phenomenon is almost universal. Everybody does it! Think about it! Why do organizations feel the need for endless and complex policies, excessive layers of approvals for often the simplest decisions, layers of management and supervision typically performing mostly non-value added work?

> *In the absence of principles, people create bureaucracy.*

When people and their full potential are fully respected, they can be taught how to hear the voice of the principles that must be considered in making good decisions. Given access to the right information and helped to understand the implications of their actions, people will almost always do the right thing. For obvious reasons reasonable limits should be placed on this trust but generally speaking, when people understand and are able to hear the voice of principles, they are capable of governing themselves.

THINK AGAIN

One last point: understanding what a principle is and the outcomes that principles govern is a lifelong study. If you think this is easy and can quickly rattle off the answers to people's questions, think again. Revisit your observations and thoughts again and again over time. Think of the onion and peel back the layers one at a time, each time trying to get deeper and deeper. Work with a trusted colleague and try to come up with the questions that cause you to think at a different level. I promise that you are not likely to ever get to the bottom and this is a good thing.

4

The Shingo Model

At the end of a successful career, the thing of greatest worth that you will leave behind will be the productive lives of countless people working in a sustainable culture of excellence based on principles!

A topic as complex as improving organizational culture is often aided by some kind of image or model. When I was Executive Director of the Shingo Institute we first tried to understand how to identify the very best of the best companies that we felt would be able to sustain their improvements over the long term. When we came to see how few of them there really were, we knew our role had to be much larger than just finding them. We knew we had to share what we were learning and support in every way possible the creation of these rare and high performing organizations. We created the Shingo Model while we were looking for a way to teach leaders and managers what we were learning.

The model helped us to summarize key insights from thought leaders and Shingo Prize recipient companies. It became clear very early on in our research that the conversations about culture we found ourselves having with executives, including values and principles, were not typical. Many senior leaders and managers struggled to understand the concepts and the relevance of what we were saying to their role as leaders. Many simply said some version of, "I am sorry; this is way too fuzzy for us. We are account-able for business results and don't have time for all of this *soft* stuff." Many others just disappeared.

We knew by then of course that there was nothing soft or fuzzy about principles or their impact on results. We just had to find a way to talk about them so that leaders could quickly see the compelling relationship between principles, systems, tools, culture and results. We needed to help them see that behaviors, especially their own, did not exist independent of results. Results are governed by principles and the voice of principles informs the ideal behaviors that lead to great results.

Changing culture is not for the faint of heart. As we observed companies attempting to do this, we realized that changing culture could be a 7–10 year journey. Ten years of anything without a roadmap was far too long; so in response to this dilemma, the Shingo Model was born!

> *Results are governed by principles and the voice of principles inform the ideal behaviors that lead to great results.*

A MODEL FOR CULTURAL TRANSFORMATION

When creating the Shingo Model we assumed that leaders have a clear business model with a sound understanding of their markets, competitors, products, economies and strategic differentiation. Given that, our focus was on what it would take to consistently execute on the business model with behaviors that could sustain excellent results over the long term.

The model was created as a way to guide leaders through the long and complex process of creating a sustainable culture of excellence and to the degree possible, accelerating this transformation. The model actually has two parts: one we called the diamond and the other we called the pyramid. This is often represented as the model and the guiding principles, as illustrated by the Shingo Institute (Figure 4.1).

THE DIAMOND

Results

On the left side of the model, results are specifically called out. Every enterprise must be able to deliver results, whether they are in the form of profits or services. An organization that has no purpose and serves no customer will eventually cease to exist.

FIGURE 4.1

The Shingo Model. (Copyright Utah State University.)

Leaders specifically and uniquely bear the greatest responsibility for creating ideal and sustainable results. When teaching the Shingo Model I like to start with results first, especially for the unconverted. Many people think that a conversation about culture is an entirely separate conversation than a conversation about results but this is an old and uninformed paradigm. Ultimately, results are a testament to the efficacy of the tools, systems, principles and culture and of course the business model of the enterprise. Everything points toward the results, be they good or bad.

A company recently asked me which principles they should focus on first. My answer surprised them. I said, "Well, which of your results are you the most concerned about and then let's work backward." If slumping sales was the biggest concern we might conduct a 5 *Whys* analysis and end up with two principles to focus on: *create value for customers* and *flow and pull value*. All counter-measure activities related to slumping sales might be directed toward:

1. Making sure that everyone understands exactly what customers want and are willing to pay for
2. Clearly documenting how every aspect of value flows through the entire enterprise
3. Identifying and targeting for improvement every barrier at every level that disrupts the continuous flow of that value

In this example, a failure to pay attention to two specific principles may be the key factors influencing the slumping sales problem. Great systems should be developed that accomplish the following:

1. Effective communications with customers
2. Translation of customer requirements into the organization
3. Creating great experiences for employees who build strong commitment to creating customer value
4. Mobilizing every employee to see barriers to flow
5. Rewards for initiative that identifies the root cause for problems and fixes them for good

All of these great systems are informed by the voice of these two principles and if heard by all and thoroughly and effectively deployed, will most certainly likely lead to a sustainable culture of customer focus. Notice that nothing on the list is really a quick fix. Getting to root cause and changing first behaviors then beliefs and values takes time and leadership. The key is that nothing about studying principles is academic. It is a practical and urgent problem solving process using real business issues as the driver.

Continuing with our examples, another disappointing result might be the excessive turnover of good employees. Again, working backward and using the 5 *Whys* tool, a team may identify the key missing principles to be *Respect for Every Individual, Lead with Humility* and *Seek Perfection*. Notice that all three principles are stated as actions that govern an outcome. Appropriate and lasting solutions might include building or improving systems that:

1. Get the senior management team out to where the work is being done by the people who are leaving.
2. Teach leaders and managers to ask good questions and listen respectfully to what people have to say.
3. Find ways to implement the ideas people have to solve the problems they experience each day.
4. Help the people with the ideas become personally engaged in implementing their own ideas.
5. Publicly and privately recognize the good work being done.
6. Provide appropriate rewards for ideal behaviors.
7. Set up scorecards that help people to see whether they are winning or losing and making a difference.

These are all examples of systems designed to create specific behavioral changes that are informed by understanding three basic principles: *Respect for Every Individual, Lead with Humility* and *Seek Perfection*.

Once the specific principle that governs the specific desired result is identified, it becomes much easier to identify an almost limitless number of behavioral improvements that can be made. Start with the results then work backwards to the principle, then the behaviors, systems and tools that affect the outcome.

Tools and Systems

Tools are enablers. To deliver great results, organizations invest in tools of all kinds. Tools are discrete techniques or methods to accomplish some kind of work. Usually tools are understood as a device or a formula or a unique item. For example a hammer is a tool, a laptop computer at some level is a tool, a job description is a tool, a paycheck is a tool. Tools exist to facilitate some useful outcome. What that outcome is and the determination of whether or not the work is useful is usually the function of a system.

Tools enable systems on the right hand of the model by helping the systems to structure work in such a way that they guide actions that are in harmony with correct principles.

A system is a complex network of tools or activities that are highly integrated to accomplish a shared objective. Systems fall into three categories: management systems, work systems and improvement systems.

Examples of management systems include systems such as strategic planning systems, performance management systems, compensation systems, communications systems, employee development systems and customer relationship management systems. These business-critical management systems get created to guide in the performance of specific tasks, the outcome of which is intended to be a certain result.

Examples of work systems include: the system for prepping a patient prior to a knee surgery, the system for reconciling and closing the books at the end of an accounting period or the system for accurately receiving and entering a customer order. These systems are highly task oriented.

Improvement systems are those systems used for problem identification and resolution, mapping the flow of customer value through an enterprise or a system to ensure that work stops immediately when a defect is identified to prevent any possible problem from reaching a customer.

An example of the relationship between systems and tools may help. To the complex system we call a smart phone the keypad is a tool. It is a specific thing that enables the system. But, a key pad is also a system, enabled by a tool called a touch key, which is in itself a complex system and so on and so on. Actually the smart phone is just a tool to enable a complex system of information management, and so it goes.

Sometimes what I describe as a tool could also be described as a subsystem. A car is a complex system that has a power train system, a chassis system, a fuel system, a coolant system, a lubricating system and an electronics system. Each of them has sub-systems. For example the coolant system has a radiator system, a distribution system, a heater system, etc. The radiator system has tools that enable it such as coils, fins, valves and a thermostat that is also a small system.

A business example might be a paycheck. Let's link the paycheck with everything related to it in the complex system we might call at some level, a compensation system. To the compensation system:

- The paycheck is a tool
- Used to reward outcomes that are part of the performance management system
- Which has in it a clear *statement* of expectations (a tool)
- That feeds into an individual employee *development plan* (a tool)
- That feeds into a performance review process (a system)
- And is part of a compensation *budget* (a tool)
- Which is the outcome of a financial *planning process* (a system)
- That is one component of a *strategic plan* (a tool)

The shared outcome of this complex system, when highly integrated, is a powerful way for clarifying what is important, transferring ownership to each individual, motivating ideal behavior and rewarding both great results and great behaviors.

Every associate must then be able to see themselves in that vision, be able to clearly articulate the value they contribute and know how to apply each of the guiding principles within the context of their work. Only when this degree of clarity and alignment exists, is an associate able to create and demonstrate both ideal behaviors and ideal results. The inclusion of purpose, strategy and especially *principles* into the articulation of systems and tools is almost never present and always powerful. We might call this alignment, when it occurs, *constancy of purpose.*

Systems and Behaviors

The system itself is easily described in statements of action. "Do this, then do this and then do this." People can see themselves doing these things. Someone has to be responsible for budgeting, someone for payroll and someone else for performance reviews, etc. Fitting the work elements and the tools all together isn't even that hard. What is hard is providing the larger context for *why* each of these steps should occur and why the work should be done in a certain way.

> *The inclusion of purpose, strategy and especially principles into the articulation of systems and tools is almost never present and always powerful.*

In most organizations, systems are created exclusively for the purpose of structuring what work is to be done and how to do it to create a specific outcome. Systems also have a powerful influence on the behaviors of people in the organization and in creating and reinforcing its culture. Every system should be designed with two key purposes in mind: first to guide the work that is to be performed, and second to guide the way people should behave in the execution of that work.

Linking systems and tools to principles provides the framework to ensure both ideal results and ideal behaviors are always achieved.

Every system should be designed with two key purposes in mind: first to guide the work that is to be performed, and second to guide the way people should behave in the execution of that work.

Principles

Sitting in the catbird seat of the model are principles. They are at the pinnacle of the model because the best way to deliver great results is to focus on the principles. Principles give voice and speak to the behavioral objectives of a system. Principles inform ideal behavior in the culture and results affirm the correctness of the principle.

Putting principles at the top of the model is what makes the Shingo philosophy unique. Every organization produces some kind of result, invests in tools, organizes work into systems and has at least some de facto culture. Principles, however, change everything. Principles inform ideal behaviors, align systems and drive results. Results, on the other hand, affirm the correctness of the principle.

In creating the Shingo Model we asked ourselves, over and over, why it is that principles almost always seemed to get lost in the deployment of the system and application of the tools? Our conclusion was that tools and systems are:

1. More tangible
2. More easily actionable
3. More broadly and easily applied
4. Lend themselves more to consulting and training models
5. Provide a plausible rationale for senior management to delegate the work of business improvement down into the organization

The danger with tools is that when they are not a part of something else with deeper meaning, they slowly disappear. Remember what the anthropologists called diffusion? This happens when organizations focus largely on the tools. If people do not understand the principle behind the tool they become prescriptive and as circumstances change the tools become less relevant and eventually become discarded. Tools are powerful when embedded into great systems and aligned with correct principles.

Tools are powerful when embedded into great systems and aligned with correct principles.

If you thought the description of the compensation system in the previous section sounded pretty good, look again. Something incredibly important is missing. You guessed it, the principles. Here are a few questions to consider in making this system even more powerful.

1. What are the ideal behaviors you want to instill into the organization?
2. What outcomes does the organization aspire to achieve and what are the principles that govern the creation of those outcomes?
3. What are the deep and abiding principles you want people to believe so that the observed and rewarded behaviors are ideal or moving towards ideal?
4. What are the high level ideal behaviors that a person doing a particular kind of work would be expected to demonstrate?
5. To what degree do the actual behaviors of the individual align with those ideal behaviors?
6. How are the current behaviors, ideal or otherwise, contributing to the ideal results required for the enterprise?

To answer many of these questions the senior management team must be very clear about the strategic direction of the enterprise and the core principles they believe are essential for creating the ideal behaviors that will lead to the required ideal results.

Principles answer for people the question of why. Why should I interact with my coworkers in a certain way? Why should I reveal every mistake that I make while doing my job? Why should I get involved in small experiments to determine if an idea can be made to work? Why should I care about what matters most to the customer? Why should I know what I specifically do to create value for customers? Why should I make the effort to understand what others around me do before and after I do my work?

Unless people know the answers to these and a hundred other questions like them, they will simply be following someone else's directions.

Powerful organizations are made up of powerful people. Powerful people are those who know what the right thing to do is and why it is right.

Principles answer for people the question of why.

Culture

At the center of the model the culture is represented. Notice that culture lies on top of everything else. As discussed earlier, other than the social or perk-based tip of the iceberg, culture is typically an afterthought and sits in the background. This way of allowing culture to just evolve results in what I called earlier as a de facto culture. A de facto culture will never accidentally, incidentally or just luckily be good enough to create world class, globally competitive organizations. By our placing culture in the center and overlapping everything else, we hoped that it would be a constant reminder that the way people behave in the workplace while doing the work has a powerful impact on everything and especially results.

> *A de facto culture will never accidentally, incidentally or luckily be good enough to create world class, globally competitive organizations.*

Culture infers behaviors and behaviors are influenced by both our beliefs and values and the systems that we operate within. Culture touches principles in the model as a reminder that our values should be grounded in principles or as Dr. Covey said, "Value Principles." Culture touches systems indicating the powerful influence systems have on the behaviors exhibited in the organization. Systems drive both results and behavior. Finally, culture overlaps tools indicating that the wise selection of good tools makes not only work more effective, but good tools can also facilitate great behavior.

USING THE MODEL TO PROVE THE PRINCIPLE

People often ask me, "How do I help convince my leaders that these principles are correct?" I usually answer by suggesting they put the principles to the test. Like a seed that can only be tested by planting, a principle can only be validated by putting it into practice. Plant it, nurture it, care for it then observe whether or not it bears fruit.

Principles inform ideal behavior in the culture and results affirm the correctness of the principle.

Here is an outline of possible actions that could be taken to test the efficacy of a principle using the Shingo Model as a guide.

1. Study the principle in detail including the foundational truth that it is based on.
2. Discuss it with others.
3. Identify the expected outcomes that carefully following the principle should lead to.
4. Identify as many ideal behaviors as you can that leaders, managers and frontline associates should demonstrate, based on the voice of the principle.
5. Align all of the systems that may impact these behaviors and the outcomes you have identified.
6. Effectively teach leaders, managers and associates how to use the best tools that enable each of these systems and build a system to ensure the tools are being both used and improved.
7. Establish metrics to be used at all levels that indicate both a change in behaviors and an improvement in the results (leading and lagging).
8. Put the metrics in a strategic and visible place on the scorecard for the enterprise and be accountable for reporting on them.
9. Lastly, discuss with others the relationship between the results and the principles; carefully study the cause and effect.

Keep the image of the model visible as you go through this and use it to discuss what you are doing and why. This process will create an experience where leaders and others can affirm for themselves the correctness of a principle. No convincing beyond that should be necessary.

THE 80/80/80 RULE

This rule of thumb may be helpful as a guide. Think about leaders, managers and associates in your organization. Now think about the concept of principles, systems and tools found in the Shingo Model.

The Leader's 80%

I have learned that leaders should generally spend 80% of their focus considering the implication of principles. This does not infer that leaders need to replace 80% of what they do, but rather that 80% of their role as leaders has direct impact on and is influenced by principles. Eighty percent of their working time represents opportunities to discuss, teach, demonstrate, reinforce and evaluate the degree to which correct principles are guiding the behaviors of other leaders, managers and every associate in every corner of the enterprise. The remaining 20% of a leader's focus is likely in some way to be on the tools and systems.

This is both a powerful idea and an extremely difficult shift for most leaders to make. Ultimately we want this 80% to become second nature; in the meantime it can be very helpful to create a simple daily management system, or in the world of "lean" it is often called leader's standard work. I have seen many tools and systems created to facilitate this 80% but the simplest system may be to consider each of the routine things that are done during the day and creating something that reminds you to consider the voice of the principles for each of them.

80% of a leader's time represents opportunities to discuss, teach, demonstrate, reinforce and evaluate the degree to which everyone in the organization is listening to the voice of the principle.

A system may be as simple as a standard template for a meeting, a reminder in your daily calendar system, a note on your door or taped to the desktop where you typically sit during meetings. It could be a request to have your assistant remind you before meetings or ask about it when you get back, it could be an agreement with all of your team members to help each other remember to consider the principles or a review at the end of each discussion of what you learned or how things changed when you considered the voice of the principle. It could also be a visual board in your office or on the wall just outside of your office where you keep track of the instances when you remembered and a note on what you learned.

This visual system will not only provide a reminder for you but will also be a statement to others who come to your office. Over time, you are likely to find that the reminder is no longer necessary as the thought process just becomes ingrained into your personal as well as the organizational culture.

The Manager's 80%

Eighty percent of a manager's focus should be on aligning systems with the voice of the principles to ensure they are driving both ideal results and ideal behaviors. Most of the organizations I have known are surprised by how much effort this new focus on systems turns out to be.

What managers need to ask themselves and others is, "What behaviors are currently being driven by the systems I am responsible for? Are the behaviors moving us closer to the voice of the principles, further away from the principles or do they have no impact on movement either way?" Each system might be evaluated from the perspective of the leader, the manager and the associates.

Evaluating and adjusting these systems so that they better drive behaviors that are more closely aligned with the voice of a principle is the work of managers. Leaders observe and ask about the systems but managers typically are doing the work. A system may be working perfectly for one of the groups but completely misaligned for others.

Most often a manager will see the need to simply modify the existing system to better align the resultant behaviors with principles. Sometimes a manager may see the need for a new system that does not currently exist or sometimes they may decide to eliminate an entire system altogether. Mangers must be perfectly in tune with the voice of the principle. They must be so familiar with the voice of principles that the ideal behaviors that the principle informs are perfectly clear to them and become the target behavior for every element of the system.

While a manager is evaluating and improving management systems, they are focusing on two things: how to better use appropriate tools inside of the systems to achieve better business results and also how to create ideal behaviors guided by the voice of a principle in leaders, managers and also frontline associates.

Managers must be so in tune with the voice of the principle that the ideal behaviors the principle speaks to become the target behavior for every element of the system.

The remaining 20% of a manager's time and attention is spent on using the tools to do their work and making sure that associates have an opportunity to understand and become committed to each of the guiding principles.

The Associate's 80%

Sadly, in many organizations there is so much chaos in the middle and at the top that many associates have learned to pretty much keep their heads down and just do their jobs.

For several years I took executives to Japan to study primarily Toyota and other companies that have tried to model themselves around the Toyota way of working. At the beginning of the trip we always visited a small training company, they call a Dojo, where trainers were some of the old production workers and managers from the years before Toyota developed the management systems we know today.

In describing the old culture, they would laugh and tell us how they used to have signals to notify each other when the top management was nearby. They talked of how they would suddenly pretend to have some deep issue taking all of their concentration and acting like they did not notice the "top brass," or suddenly they would need a tool that would take them away from their machine. Others said that they simply hid behind their machine until they were gone. At no cost would they risk having a direct conversation with top management. All they wanted was to be left alone.

Fortunately, Toyota began to understand what they were sacrificing as a consequence of their culture of fear and made the tough journey of changing top management behaviors. Toyota is a very good example of how this transformation can be done and also a model of what it takes to keep a principle from evaporating over time.

Frontline workers are the lifeblood of any organization. Their primary role is to execute the management systems, work systems and improvement systems of the enterprise. Frontline workers may be bank tellers, nurses, data entry clerks, engineers, designers, custodians, machine operators or perhaps even doctors. This usually means they are using appropriate tools to get their work done. These tools may be physical tools such as computers, machines, instruments, forms or checklists, or they may be problem-solving tools such as histograms, Pareto charts, fishbone diagrams or value stream maps. Often, frontline associates will use existing or invent their own tools to help them do or improve the way they do their jobs.

Frontline workers are the lifeblood of any organization. Their primary role is to use all appropriate tools to execute the management, work and improvement systems of the enterprise.

This use of tools may consume up to 80% of an associate's time and attention. The remaining 20% is used studying and applying principles to their work and making recommendations for improvements to the work and management systems that affect their contribution.

Obviously the 80/80/80 Rule is a rule of thumb but is a good benchmark for evaluating the degree to which leaders, managers and associates are doing the things that will move the culture closer to a sustainable culture of enterprise excellence based on principles.

THE PYRAMID

The second half of what at the time we called the Shingo Model was the pyramid. The pyramid was how we chose to organize and display the ten principles that ultimately became a part of the model.

Much of the remainder of this book will focus on describing each of these categories, the principles within them and how the voice of each principle informs the creation of a sustainable culture of enterprise excellence. A deeper understanding of how the principles came to be understood and organized the way they were may be helpful at this point.

Along with a team of my trusted colleagues at the Shingo Prize at Utah State University, we began an earnest search to understand how it was possible that so many companies could receive the Shingo Prize but then in the ensuing years regress so significantly. We had heard others speak of and we had read a great deal about similar experiences with recipients of the Malcolm Baldrige National Quality award. Since we were closest to the Shingo Prize, we chose to focus our analysis on companies that had either received or almost received the Shingo Prize but then regressed.

We hypothesized that one or more of five possibilities existed:

1. Our examiners were not sufficiently competent to be able to see the reality.
2. The companies were experts at hiding the truth.
3. They really were that good at the time we did the assessment but something traumatic happened to them after.
4. We didn't ask the right questions.
5. We were looking for the wrong things.

In the end, we concluded that several of these possible causes described above had some impact on sustainability but the largest single cause came down to number five. We were plain and simple looking for the wrong things. The Shingo Prize criteria, as continues to be the case for most recognition programs in the world, was focused on looking for evidence of the existence of improvement programs and the application of generally accepted tools of improvement. If these things were broadly enough practiced, and the management team was mostly supportive, the organization would receive the Shingo Prize.

What we did not focus on was the degree to which the fundamental concepts or principles behind those programs and tools were deeply embedded into the belief system, thinking and daily practices of every employee, from top-to-bottom and side-to-side. In short, we were not evaluating the existing culture of the organization. We were looking for outward signs of good things not the inward drivers behind what we were seeing. We were looking only at the top of the iceberg not the massive structure below the waterline.

GATHERING THE PRINCIPLES

Using this insight from the Shingo Prize and the hundreds of companies that had been evaluated, we embarked on a many months-long process to learn everything that thought leaders over the last 50 years had taught about creating enterprise excellence. As we went through a thorough study of their books, videos, consulting models, etc. we kept asking ourselves is what we were seeing a tool, a system or a foundational principle. We sorted through everything we could find to discover the principles or the core concepts each thought leader was trying to teach.

As we studied the work of these thought leaders we began to notice a few "red threads" that ran through and connected much of what they said. These themes began to emerge over and over. No one person represented every principle, but little by little we were able to teach ourselves to look past the outward and obvious and focus on the principles.

Once we knew what to look for we discovered that in most books the overarching principles were usually described in the first chapter. Succeeding chapters often went on to teach about the tools and systems that flowed from them. Eventually, after soliciting the help of dozens of

FIGURE 4.2
Principles identified in the Shingo Model. (Copyright Utah State University.)

our trusted colleagues from many parts of the world, we boiled it down to ten key unique principles.

Dr. Shigeo Shingo said that principles should be organized into "buckets" or categories. Here are the categories or buckets of principles we concluded represented the best knowledge from the most trusted thought leaders on the topic of Operational or Enterprise Excellence.

The pyramid (Figure 4.2) is how we represented these principles and their categories, or buckets, in the Shingo Model.

CULTURAL ENABLERS

Our research revealed two key principles that best enable a sustainable culture of excellence: *Respect Every Individual* and *Lead with Humility*. These two foundational principles are mandatory for the kind of organizational culture that ultimately enables the full potential of every single associate. They are the hardest to fully embrace and also the most impactful.

These enabling principles of *Respect Every Individual* and *Lead with Humility* are at the bottom of the pyramid representing foundational principles. An organization made up of people can never achieve sustainable excellence without recognizing that the strength of the organization comes not from the few people at the top but rather from the combined competency and commitment of every single person in the organization.

This mindset of humility and respect enable the full potential of any organization to create greatness.

At the end of a successful career, the thing of greatest worth that you will leave behind will be the productive lives of countless people working in a sustainable culture of excellence based on principles!

CONTINUOUS IMPROVEMENT

The five principles we identified that relate to continuous improvement are: *Seek Perfection, Embrace Scientific Thinking, Focus on Process, Assure Quality at the Source,* and *Flow and Pull Value.* These are five key operational principles that directly affect any organization's ability to focus improvement efforts.

Notice that each one is stated in the form of an action, a rule or a natural law. These are the things that you do to create improvement. When your actions are guided by the voice of these five principles, you get a certain and predictable outcome. For example, when you *Seek Perfection* you create a mindset in the organization of continuous improvement. Seeking for perfection results in a healthy dissatisfaction in the status quo and a recognition that there is always a better way of doing everything.

ENTERPRISE ALIGNMENT

Two critical principles fell into this category, *Think Systemically* and *Create Constancy of Purpose.* Both of these principles, when embraced broadly by a culture, result in the confidence of both individuals and teams to take initiative and know that what they are doing is moving the organization closer to its vision and will work together for the good of the whole.

Both of these principles, when embraced broadly by a culture, result in the confidence of both individuals and teams to take initiative and know that what they are doing is moving the organization closer to its vision and will work together for the good of the whole.

RESULTS

Create Value for Customers is the principle at the top of the pyramid, representing the pinnacle objective of any organization. Value creation for customers is the ultimate measurement of results. Balanced scorecards include good metrics related to Quality, Cost, Delivery and often the morale of people and should reflect both key performance indicators as well as key behavioral indicators. *Creating Value for Customers* must ultimately be the true north for any organization.

While all of these principles are critical in creating a sustainable culture of excellence, I have learned that leaders must pay particular attention to the cultural enablers. These are the principles that enable continuous improvement, enterprise alignment and ultimately great results.

5

Respect Every Individual

A personal mentor once told me that anybody can respect everybody, but almost nobody can respect every single body.

THE VOICE OF THE PRINCIPLE ...
RESPECT EVERY INDIVIDUAL

Few principles speak with such a clear voice, as does the principle of *Respect for Every Individual*. There is almost nothing that a leader, manager or frontline associate can do in the workplace that has a more immediate, positive and profound impact on the contribution of others than does the demonstration of respect for every single person. Carl Rogers, in describing the "Person-Centered Approach" to leadership, described this principle as having "unconditional positive regard." (Carl Rogers, 1980)

> *The first step in showing respect is to have respect. Any attempt to demonstrate respect that is not genuine will ultimately fail.*

Treating someone with respect, even in the face of a complex problem, creates the conditions where solutions not only become visible but also possible. Treating every individual with respect speaks to the character of the person showing respect and builds character in the person being respected.

When the principle of respect for every individual is deeply embedded into a culture, the voice of this principle informs behaviors that enable the full potential of every individual associate as well as the combined power of the entire enterprise. When respect speaks, it speaks to the heart of people. The voice of this principle is heard not only at the moment respect is shown but echoes days, weeks and months later. After graduating from university and completing my first major project, the senior manager three levels up sent a note home to my wife informing her of the good work I had done and letting her know how much he appreciated having me in his department. Now 42 years later, I still feel warmth for this man. I consider *Respect for Every Individual* to be the foundational or enabling principle of all ten principles of Enterprise Excellence identified in the Shingo Model and discussed in this book.

Years ago I learned a powerful lesson related to this principle. My administrative assistant's husband was diagnosed with abdominal cancer. He was about 38 years old and they had two small children. I consulted with corporate HR to determine what options existed for supporting her as he struggled for life and she planned for the future of her family. I was shocked to learn that the options were very limited and in fact were quite explicit about what I could and could not do. As he got worse I knew she would need to be by his side full-time for what time he had left but I also knew this would not be supported if I asked for permission.

In the end, I just decided that I would do whatever it took to help her get through this tough time and that I would deal with any fallout that might occur. Even though she ended up being out for almost two full months, the impact of this small demonstration of respect for not only her but also her husband and children ended up having a huge impact far beyond her small family.

Everyone of course became aware of what was being done and pitched in to make sure that her absence did not have any negative impact on our results. In fact, people began to show more respect for each other, people began to become aware of other people's personal situations at home and at work and the overall morale and productivity of our group and several other groups around us increased significantly. When she returned to work, her passion for our mission and commitment to the company was noticed by everyone and impacted the performance of many. The Voice of the Principle spoke of compassion, loyalty, teamwork and commitment. Respect was the enabler.

I was a young man when I first heard the term **respect** articulated in the context of business. Someone was talking about the Toyota management system when they said that Respect for People was one of their basic philosophies. Since then I have heard this statement expressed in many different ways including just "Respect," "Respect for humanity" or "Respect for people."

When working with senior leaders, I have found that when articulated at such a high level almost everyone universally agrees. Who can't agree with the idea of respect? Saying you respect all of humanity however invokes almost no controversy and creates very little debate or self-reflection. It is easy to say, "Of course, I respect everyone." Yet very few people can say with conviction that they respect every single person. There is a big difference between *humanity* and *every single person*.

There is a big difference between humanity and every single person.

Most normal people begin instantly to put caveats on the kinds of people they probably don't really respect, like the person who is always late for work, the person who doesn't seem to care about what they do or maybe the person who always disagrees with everything they hear. Many people say, "How can I respect someone who just doesn't care or someone who I simply do not trust?"

Other categories of individuals who are frequently named as not worthy of being respected are those who are obviously not as smart as me or who think they are smarter than me; or someone whose skin is a different color than mine or has a very different ethnic background; or someone who was not educated like me or who is not as experienced as me; or someone who thinks they have all of the answers; or someone who is not nearly at as high a level as I am; or someone who values very different things than I do.

This is where it starts to get real and tough. This is where the real world has a significant impact on the "degree to which" an individual can say that they really have genuine respect for every single person.

It is very dangerous to let our own personal values influence our judgment of the rightness or wrongness of someone else's values. When we judge in this way, we create barriers between us and those we seek to help. This is particularly important for leaders and managers seeking to improve the quality of results through building sustainable cultures of excellence. Not only are our values very personal and influenced by our life experiences, but so are everyone else's. To create a great organizational culture that is capable of consistently delivering ideal results, leaders must learn to respect people for who they are then provide experiences that help them learn to value new things that are grounded in the voice of guiding principles.

When we think that our differences make us *better than* rather than just *different from* others, divisiveness enters into an organization and human potential is always sacrificed as a consequence. The only fair standard for evaluating personal values is through the lens of a principle. The voice of a principle is impartial and non-judgmental and can far more perfectly inform our approach to improving ourselves and others.

> *When we think that our differences make us **better than** rather than just **different from**, divisiveness enters an organization and human potential is always sacrificed.*

I worked with a company once that was located in a small, reasonably isolated community in the South Central part of the United States. Most of the 250 employees were unable to finish high school, did not have good access to a quality healthcare system and a great many were the product of homes where parents were either unemployed or significantly underemployed.

When we first began our efforts to improve the culture of the organization I was taken back by the disrespectful way the workforce was described by a few key members of the senior management team. Each time we discussed options for making improvements, we were confronted with hugely disparaging comments about the people's inability or unwillingness to participate in or even to accept the ideas being discussed. Most of this mindset came from one key leader who had been with the organization for many years but whose prejudice also had a very large impact on nearly everyone else.

I worked with the leadership team for over 18 months helping them to become more principled in their leadership. As we worked to better understand and deploy each of the principles associated with Enterprise Excellence we kept coming back to the principle of *Respect Every Individual*. No matter what room we were in (figuratively), it was always the elephant that constrained our progress. Little by little the team began to change their thinking and commitment to change; all that is, but the one main individual who held the key to the organization. In private conversations with me he acknowledged that in his heart he knew he was wrong to think the way he did but felt that after so many years, he was fundamentally unable to change. In the end, this good man left the company of his own choice.

One other time a similar thing happened in a company where I was employed. The Sr. Vice President of one of the key business groups of the company was 65 years old when we began our work to improve the culture. His office was right next to mine and we spent many long evenings when most people had gone home, discussing the changes he felt he would have to make for this to work. He told me many times that it would be much easier to just retire.

The interesting thing was that outside of the workplace, this leader's behavior was entirely different than it was in the office. People loved to be with him and fought to be on his golf team even though he was a terrible golfer. He had a handicapped daughter whom he was devoted to and demonstrated enormous compassion for her and others who had her disabilities.

As our discussions got deeper and deeper, he realized that his work culture was much different than his life culture and that he liked his non-work way of being far better. Over a couple of years and before he did retire, I had the pleasure of watching this leader work very hard to develop congruency between who he was and how he behaved at work. I know it was not easy for him but without doubt the last few years of his work were his most productive and fulfilling. His comments at his retirement party, of course at the golf club, were very moving to everyone.

Politics and Respect

Political differences have become much more than just differences. It seems that respect for the uniqueness of political opposition has been completely replaced with anger, bitterness and even more often, hatred. Imagine how great a political leader would be if they were truly able to demonstrate genuine respect for "every single constituent" no matter how similar or different they were. By respecting each other, communities could again become melting pots of people from very different backgrounds. The differences in individual values would be celebrated as a way to see and solve complex problems more effectively. What a powerful force for good a political leader who possessed genuine respect for every single individual could be in the world. The same is true for the leaders of organizations.

What a powerful force for good a political leader that possessed genuine respect for every single individual could be in the world.

Learning to have and demonstrate respect for every individual is the first step in empowering the creation of a sustainable culture of excellence. This principle, like all others, is a statement of action that is based on a foundational truth. Those who understand the principle well enough to hear its voice can begin to demonstrate ideal behaviors.

When we demonstrate ideal behaviors we can expect a certain outcome...it is predictable. This applies regardless the level of management you work at, regardless the person you are showing respect for or regardless where in the world you live. The outcomes are predictable.

THE FOUNDATIONAL TRUTH ...
RESPECT EVERY INDIVIDUAL

For a leader, understanding and believing in the fundamental goodness of human nature is central to changing our personal beliefs about the people we work with, leading them toward better behaviors and ultimately building a sustainable culture of enterprise excellence.

The discussion of human nature is central to changing our personal beliefs about people, leading them toward better behaviors and ultimately building a sustainable culture of enterprise excellence.

This conversation may be very challenging for many people. If you have trouble, be patient, set aside your feelings, push pause and consider other options. Our goal is to learn to hear the voice of the principle *Respect Every Individual*. The clearer this voice becomes, the more likely we are to change our perspective of why people do what they do at work. Understanding and respecting these differences gives leaders and managers many more options for how to reshape beliefs, values and personal behaviors. Any hope of transforming corporate culture depends on our ability to change beliefs and behaviors. It is simply not practical to just terminate everyone who behaves in the workplace in less than an ideal way.

Rob Galloway, President of US Synthetic, once said to me, that "You simply cannot hire and fire your way into excellence. Somewhere along the line you have to lead, nurture and enable the development of people to help them become better." For most of us our only play is the hand we were dealt and assisting every individual to reach their full potential is not only the right thing to do it is the smart thing to do. On the other hand, creating a values centric recruiting and on-boarding system is a proactive way to improve our starting point.

> *You simply cannot hire and fire your way into excellence. Somewhere along the line you have to lead, nurture and enable the development of people to help them become better.*

To truly hear the voice of the principle we need to uncover the foundational truth that sits below the principle. When we understand the foundational truth that the principle is based on we begin to understand the *why* behind the principle. As with almost everything, understanding *why* prepares people to make better behavioral decisions. A foundational truth has always been true and always will be; therefore if the principle is properly grounded in it, the outcomes become predictable.

> *A foundational truth has always been true and always will be; therefore if the principle is properly grounded in it, the outcomes become predictable.*

In the classroom I ask small teams of corporate leaders to brainstorm the question, "Why should we respect *every* individual?" Their assignment is to boil down all of their conversation into a simple sentence or phrase that answers that question. The first time they do this it is not an easy task. The temptation always is to first answer the question from the perspective of what outcomes do you want to achieve. Managers and leaders are already thinking about how the principle governs outcomes or results. The results they describe are almost always about the business, meaning: if I treat people in a certain way, then they will most certainly give me more of what I want, in this case, results for the business.

Improving business results is not a bad aspiration but not a high enough reason to treat someone with genuine respect. The motivation to treat someone in a respectful way because I want to get something out of it is shallow, selfish and almost always seen as disingenuous. Respect cannot be about me, it must always be about the other person. Of course, good things happen when people are treated with respect but that cannot become the motivation.

Foundational truths are just what they say, foundational. They sit on the cause side of the principle not on the effect side. Another way of saying it is that they sit underneath the principle. The reason why I treat someone with respect, for it to be respectful, must be entirely about the other person.

The reason why I treat someone with respect, for it to be respectful, must be entirely about the other person.

The reason why we should respect every individual is twofold:

1. Because every single person has intrinsic value, and
2. Because every individual has unrealized potential.

Intrinsic Value

Value is inherent in every human being and is not something that people have to earn. Because they are not rocks, machines, buildings or any other inanimate object, they deserve our respect. We respect their humanity and as a fellow human I should treat them in a certain way. On the surface this idea seems reasonable but in reality it is quite complicated. For example there is a difference between respecting them as human beings and respecting them for some great attribute they have developed, such as I respect their ability to facilitate a team through a complex situation, or I respect their integrity, their ability to think strategically or their ability to turn an idea into action.

These are examples of specific things that a person may have accomplished that have earned for them the respect of others. This is not the kind of respect I am talking about. Universal respect for every single person is a gift that comes with being human. It is not earned by some act of greatness it is simply innate to all of us. Every single person, every single member of our organization or enterprise deserves our respect simply because they are. Learning to show our feelings of respect, even when people's behavior is far less than ideal, is the challenge. The first step in showing respect is to have respect. Any attempt to demonstrate respect that is not genuine will ultimately fail.

One of my favorite lines from a movie was in "The Man From Snowy River." When Jessica, the daughter, encouraged a friend to ride her father's very expensive and untrained Black Stallion without permission, her Father lost his temper, said some things he shouldn't have and slapped her. The aunt who witnessed this exchange said, "You would never have killed the spirit of that stallion the way you just did your own daughter."

Sometimes we thoughtlessly place greater value in things than we do people. The test of the sincerity of our respect comes when things go wrong, or when someone's behavior is far less than ideal; what we do at that point makes all of the difference. My mother used to say to me when I was raising my children, "love the child, not the behavior." I think this is sage advice when studying the principle of respect for every individual: "respect the person, not the thing that the person is doing." Because we always respect people as human beings the way we deal with their poor performance or incompetency or even insubordination should be done in a way that shows respect.

Strength through Respect

Respect means being willing to confront difficult issues and appropriately act on them for the good of the larger group. Poor performance that is allowed to go unchecked is disrespectful to everyone, including the person with the bad performance. Leaders who demonstrate respect help people to see the reality of their poor performance, make a sincere effort to help them improve but also have the greater good in mind. Respect means telling the truth and doing the hard thing when necessary.

Often demonstrating respect is misinterpreted as being soft or weak. This could not be further from the truth. I worked for a man once who could not make decisions for fear of hurting someone's feelings. I remember sitting around a conference table for hours, often with 12–15 very valuable people in the room. We would go around and around, over and over on issues with no one willing to just make a decision. We would often get to the point where even the most hardnosed people would be willing to give up their point of view if someone would just make a decision. This unwillingness or inability to either lead the group to consensus or simply decide and act was disrespectful to everyone in the room. Showing respect takes courage and decisiveness.

Untapped Potential

Nearly all of my friends who are about my age agree that one of the best parts of getting older is becoming a grandparent. For me, this is true for several reasons. First, because you get to see your children as adults;

and second, because they experience for themselves many of the same things that were hard for you.

Some of the best advice I give my children who have children is that they are not raising children, they are raising adults. When they become frustrated by a childish behavior we encourage them to think carefully about what they want that child to become before deciding how to act. Children have infinitely more potential than the tears and other unpleasant stuff that presents itself immediately upon delivery. Decisions about how to act as a parent must be based not on what you see now but what you see well into the future.

This metaphor applies for all of us. Not only do people have intrinsic value but they also have a huge reservoir of untapped potential. The miraculous thing is that no matter how much or how little a person accomplishes in life, the reservoir of potential remains far more full than empty. Because this is true for everyone, what we are learning to respect is not just someone's current capabilities or performance but we are respecting every single person's ability to continue to grow and develop, almost limitlessly. Similarly, when we waste a person's time at work, we are wasting far more than just who they are at the moment.

> *The miraculous thing is that no matter how much or how little a person accomplishes in life, the reservoir of potential remains far more full than empty.*

Just like the parent to the child, this thought takes a lot of pressure off of leaders and managers and illustrates why you can't just hire and fire your way into success. No one has all of the current capabilities needed to succeed; they must be developed and nurtured over time, often a very long time. Lying fallow in every single one of your employees lies the untapped potential to increase productivity by 20% per year, reduce costs by 10% per year or decrease by half the time required to successfully introduce great new products and services to your customers.

If these and a hundred more outstanding outcomes made possible by the release of people's untapped potential sound great to you, think again about the ultimate best outcome that can come. It is not about the enterprise or some value you as a leader might obtain but the best outcome comes to the individual who is growing and learning how to contribute more and more of their potential.

I remember with incredible pride how it felt to stand and watch a machine operate that was being controlled by a program that I had written. Creating this program was not natural for me and very difficult to do but in the doing, something great happened and I became much more valuable to my employer. Even though developing the potential of every employee has the greatest value for the person, make no mistake that everyone else benefits as well.

In summary, the foundational truth behind why we respect every individual is because everyone has intrinsic value and untapped potential. Stated slightly differently, because everyone has intrinsic value and untapped potential, therefore we respect every individual. Intrinsic value and untapped potential is the reason why we respect.

I invite every reader to discuss this principle and consider other possible foundational truths that may influence why we should respect every individual.

IDEAL BEHAVIORS THAT FLOW FROM THE VOICE OF THE PRINCIPLE

The more deeply a person understands a principle and the foundational truths that make it universal and timeless, the more likely are their behaviors to be moving closer and closer towards ideal. Even though there are many examples of ideal behavior associated with this principle, I will list a few to help guide your thinking.

Leaders

1. When talking with an employee, a leader always looks them in the eye, uses their name if possible, listens with real intent, asks meaningful questions, reinforces good results and behavior and thanks them for their specific work.
2. Leaders make sure that every associate has the knowledge, skill, information and time required to complete their work to the required standard.
3. Leaders routinely talk about respect and challenge others to consider the degree to which respect for every individual is being demonstrated in the actions being taken.

Managers

1. Managers do not allow an associate's bad behavior to go unchecked. They coach, mentor and demonstrate ideal behavior, but ultimately expect every associate to be moving their behaviors closer and closer towards ideal.

2. Managers avoid the temptation to provide solutions to associate problems. Rather, they ask questions, coach and support individuals and teams in their own diagnosis of root cause and implementation of appropriate countermeasures.

3. Every manager is constantly evaluating the degree to which the systems being used reflect the voice of this principle and are driving ideal behaviors throughout the organization that demonstrate respect for every single person.

Associates

1. Associates ask sincere questions and listen to managers and senior leaders to genuinely understand strategy, policy and direction. They assume positive intent but also ask appropriate hard questions.

2. Associates support their colleagues in solving problems they may have had previous experience with.

Countless ideal behaviors can be described relating to every specific element of work. The temptation for leaders as they begin to hear the voice of this principle is to create lists of expected ideal behaviors for others that become new management expectations. I have learned over time that this process is in itself disrespectful. What works best is when leaders articulate high level expectations similar to the examples identified above but what that looks like in every part of the organization will no doubt be very different.

The role of leaders is to teach every associate how to hear the voice of the principle and then trust them to identify the ideal behaviors they believe are most appropriate for their work. Managers should create a system that requires everyone to routinely evaluate and elevate their expectations of ideal behaviors that speak to this principle.

If *Respect Every Individual* is on one side of a coin, then *Lead with Humility* is on the other. These two principles are so closely connected that you cannot have one without the other. The next chapter will detail the principle on the other side of the coin.

6

Lead with Humility

The most powerful place to begin the process of cultural transformation is with leaders focusing first on their own behaviors.

THE VOICE OF THE PRINCIPLE ... *LEAD WITH HUMILITY*

The principle of *Lead with Humility* is also, like *Respect for Every Individual*, one of the key enablers of cultural transformation. Humility brings with it teachability, and learning to hear the voice of any principle requires teachability. It means being willing to consider the possibility of something new, something important that might fundamentally change your way of thinking and acting. For most of us, if we are being honest with ourselves, this is frightening.

Leading with humility runs counter to most graduate school training and leadership courses. A great many individuals who eventually find themselves in senior management positions are the product of de facto cultures that evolve to reinforce aggressive, very confident (if not over confident) experts who have demonstrated a relentless pursuit of numbers and results. These attributes often work contrary to the development of humility in a leader.

In James Collins' book, *Good to Great*, he described a seldom talked about and profound difference between good leaders and great leaders, what he called, level five leaders (Collins 2001). The attribute that all of the greatest leaders possessed is humility. Collins described leaders with humility as, "modest and willful, shy and fearless." David A. Bednar said, "Humility is not thinking less of yourself, it is thinking less about yourself." This chapter will explore many key aspects of what it means and what it takes to lead with humility.

Leading with humility may be one of the toughest principles to apply. By definition, leading with humility is deeply personal and becoming a humble leader is a kind of "chicken or the egg" process. It takes humility to see the value of understanding the principle (the chicken), yet it is by listening to the voice of this principle (the egg) that the conditions can be created for humility to be developed. This is a situation where I often say to leaders who are caught between these two positions, "Let's conduct an experiment with humility and see what the outcome is. Let the fruit of the experiment be the proof of the correctness of the principle." We then craft an experiment, usually with the help of a trusted advisor, that will reveal the outcomes of humility and create personal experiences that may begin to change long-held mindsets and leadership style. Later in this chapter I will tell you of such an experiment I was asked to facilitate and its outcomes.

The obvious problem with this experiment is that humility is not an action, it is a way of being. Humility that is manufactured will be tolerated by others only long enough to determine whether or not it is real. Artificial humility can only be acted out for so long, then inevitably something will happen and the real person is revealed. How then can humility be developed when it does not exist naturally?

Humility that is manufactured will be tolerated by others only long enough to determine whether or not it is real.

When I work with leadership teams we always solidify a new behavioral concept by going to where work actually gets done by the actual people who do it. In Japan they call this place the "Gemba". Because the Gemba is so important to seeing reality, perhaps, a short description will be helpful. It comes from two Japanese kanji characters which when translated mean "Gem", or the place where something occurs, and "ba" which means the people who do it. The Gemba is where everything happens; it is where you see reality. Problems are always better understood and better solutions identified at the Gemba.

The Gemba is where everything happens; it is where you see reality. Problems are always better understood and better solutions identified at the Gemba.

I was with a leadership team once that after almost a year of work with me and five or six successive rounds of conference room learning followed by observations at the *Gemba*, I felt they were finally becoming quite skilled at observing and describing behaviors of people in the workforce. Because I believed they were ready for the graduate course, I asked, "I wonder what 'your' behaviors are, as the senior leadership team in this company that could be causing people to act the way they do?" What I wanted was for each individual leader to ask the question, "What am I doing that could be causing others in the organization to behave the way they do?"

The most powerful place to begin the process of cultural transformation is with leaders focusing first on their own behaviors. You are the easiest person to influence, and fixing yourself is likely to have a far greater impact on others than anything else you can do. Confronting the realities of your own behaviors is best done at your own *Gemba*, not in a classroom or conference room or even your office. Your perspective of reality will change when you are physically with the actual people who do the work, in the place where the actual work is done.

Seeing the truth about how your own behaviors are contributing to the behaviors of others is something that must be heard with your heart and not your head. This means you can't become a leader who leads with humility while reading a book in your office, on an airplane or participating in a conference. Becoming a humble leader must happen experientially and must be felt by doing not by reading or listening. When we discuss the foundational truth related to this principle this idea will become more clear.

> *You are the easiest person to influence, and fixing yourself is likely to have a far greater impact on others than anything else you can do.*

SEEING REALITY

Leading with Humility requires great self-awareness, not from your own point of view but from the point of view of others who see you as you really are. Very often, being able to see what others see and hear what they may have to say requires at a minimum curiosity and patience but ultimately great humility. This is indeed another chicken or the egg issue, so the only way to do it is to just start; a small experiment again is usually the safest approach. The experiment however must not be too safe or it will not create the depth of experience that will result in a change. The old adage "No pain no gain" applies perfectly to this situation.

In the beginning, people may be very reluctant to tell you the truth, so stay with it. Do not assume that what people say first is at the root; keep going and dig deeper. Be sincere, be open, be curious and be grateful for the feedback people are willing to share. I have learned that for me the best way to deal with this kind of feedback is to be totally congruent with how I am feeling, and if possible, be congruent publicly. This means that if it hurts to hear something, go ahead and say what you are feeling: "Hearing that really hurts. I never supposed that when I did 'x' it would have that kind of an impact," or, "I am shocked to just be coming to this insight after so long. What have I done that has made it so hard for any of you to tell me this earlier?" Make sure that your inquiry is always about you, not them.

Max DePree, past CEO of Herman Miller, Inc. said, "Your first responsibility as a leader is to see reality, the last is to say thank you. In between, the leader is a servant" (DePree 1987). If your leadership does not begin from a clear sense of reality, the likelihood of having genuine followers is very small.

Understanding the truth about how your own behaviors are contributing to the bad behaviors of others is something that must be heard with your heart and not your head.

Because it was so meaningful to me, I would like to repeat a short story I shared near the end of the chapter one. A few years ago I had a rude awakening when two nominated representatives of my own team came to me in private and said, "Bob, you travel four days a week then come blasting into the office on Friday morning and after a few pleasantries, go into your conference room, close the door and meet with your direct reports for most of the day. Yes, you are friendly enough and smile and wave when passing our offices but almost never do you sit down and just ask how we are doing. You rarely ask us to show you the things we are working on and are most proud of. We are very disappointed that you do not practice what you are teaching."

Wow! Talk about a rude awakening. How could the guy who teaches this stuff every week get it so wrong! My own behavior was sending all of the wrong messages and creating distance between my great employees and me. After working through the classic steps of surprise, anger, rejection and finally getting to acceptance, I realized that I always said I valued my frontline associates, and I think I really did, but my actual behavior said that I really valued the time with my direct reports even more.

Your first responsibility as a leader is to see reality. Failing that, the likelihood of having genuine followers is very small.

Confronting tough realities might be an excellent time to have a trusted advisor sitting in the chair next to you. This should be someone whose feedback you value and trust to tell you the truth no matter how hard it is to hear. One role of this advisor might be to help you ask questions that will generate the best feedback and then help you to listen with real intent and unconditional positive regard for the giver.

Earlier in my career, after completing an annual 360-degree performance evaluation, I was trying to deal with an important feedback point indicating my inability to effectively solicit and listen to the input of all team members. This was a serious piece of information that was very difficult for me to hear. I was a vice president in the company at that time and the suggestion was made by my leader that perhaps I could have someone from outside the company help me to understand and fix this problem. As hard as it was, I took his advice. On the first day that this "trusted advisor" was with me he sat in the back of a conference room during a particularly important team meeting where we were dealing with a very complex problem. He was very quiet; actually he never said a word but had his head down, apparently just noodling on a note pad and constantly looking at his watch for almost two hours. I remember being quite perturbed.

After the meeting we went back to my office and I was going to really give it to him, but before I could he opened a picture he had drawn of the conference room showing me relative to every other person in the room. His "noodles" were actually lines and numbers showing who was speaking, who they were speaking to and the amount of time occupied by the speaker. I gulped, suspecting immediately where this was going. What the map revealed was that over the course of the two hours, roughly 80% of the communications centered on me and was directed to about 20% of the people in the room. My trusted advisor then said, "Bob, you need to reverse those numbers. Less than 20% of the communications should come from you and more than 80% needs to come from all of the other members of your team." How could I argue, the numbers were right there in front of me and as painful as it was, I knew he was right. Without his help I was incapable of seeing the truth about myself.

Only from a clear understanding of reality can a leader create the personal transformation that will result in a cultural transformation of the organization.

I love the image of a kitten looking in the mirror and seeing a lion (Figure 6.1). I think the originator of this image intended it to be about self-esteem but it could also represent the need for us to be honest with ourselves about our strengths and weaknesses. If you see yourself as a roaring lion, king of the jungle, but others see you as a weak pussycat, you may be in for a rude awakening at some point when you look back and no one is following. See reality! This issue is not so much about who you are, as it is your willingness and ability to see the truth. Only from a clear understanding of reality can a leader create the personal transformation that will result in a cultural transformation of the organization.

I have a very close friend who is the CEO of a very successful consumer products manufacturing company. He asked me to help him learn to be

FIGURE 6.1
Seeing reality. (By license agreement.)

honest with himself, and to do it in front of his employees. One day in a very important and strategic meeting, I called him out on something that he kept doing. I had actually seen this behavior many times but in this case it was particularly damaging to the group process and the outcome of the meeting was so important. I named the specific behavior that he was exhibiting and told him how I thought this behavior was impacting the group's ability to move forward. Naturally the room went deathly silent. My friend looked straight at me, blanched, paused for several seconds, then blushed and finally said, "OK Bob, now seems like a very good time for me to learn something that I think is probably very important. Let's talk about it!"

The ensuing discussion that eventually encompassed everyone in the room was powerful and life changing, not just for the CEO but also for everyone else humble enough to see themselves in the conversation. Such demonstrations of humility, courage and ideal behavior from a leader become both the fuel for and the legends of cultural transformation.

Demonstrations of humility, courage and ideal behavior from a leader become both the fuel for and the legends of cultural transformation.

I have observed numerous recipients of the Shingo Prize who were shocked that they actually received it when all they could see were the gaps between where they thought they were and the standard. Conversely, the leaders of many organizations who have challenged for the prize and did not receive it have become angry and bitter, critical of examiners, suspicious of the criteria or disappointed in the Shingo Institute. They believed they were far better than the final report indicated. When this bitterness was expressed to us, we always felt terrible for the people and the organization but the phone calls were in fact an affirmation that we had indeed done the right thing. The leader's lack of humility always became evident and impacted the examiners just as it did the actual culture of the organization being evaluated. The biblical saying, "By their fruits ye shall know them" always seemed apropos.

THE FOUNDATIONAL TRUTH ... *LEAD WITH HUMILITY*

To understand *why* we should lead with humility it will help to explore the foundational truth that sits below the principle. Remember, the principle is a statement of action that governs an outcome that is predictable.

The thing that makes it predictable is that the principle is based on a foundational truth. It is the foundational truth a principle is based on that makes it universal, timeless and self-evident. (This relationship is so important to understanding the voice of a principle that I will repeat it many times in subsequent chapters.)

The reason why we lead with humility is not so that more people will like us, or so that people will give us more of their ideas or even so that that we will have a more stable workforce. These are all natural outcomes of leading with humility but they are not the reason why. These outcomes sit above the principle and are an effect, not a cause.

A foundational truth exists below the principle and is the reason why we should lead with humility; it is the cause that leads to the effect. The foundational truth must be something that is foundational and true for all people at all times. I heard a plant manager say recently when asked to describe a principle, "A principle is based on truth that cannot be denied!" I was so proud of him! It is only a foundational truth if it provides efficacy to the principle.

Most experienced managers and leaders have learned that when hiring a new college graduate they come to the job with almost no experience. Everything they do they are doing for the very first time. I remember what this felt like when I went to work for John Deere after receiving my Bachelor's Degree. I had never worked in a large factory, never done real engineering work, never been a part of a real team, never had a real boss in an industrial setting and never been accountable for a real outcome that was actually important. I wanted so much to appear confident in the eyes of my manager and peers but inside I was terrified. I suspect that all of the new recruits felt exactly the same as I did.

Somehow most of us made it through. Most of us gained a few scars along the way and some of us received many of them. Our ignorance created a very steep learning curve. I remember pouring over old textbooks for similar case studies, looking for similar problems from class notes to the ones I now confronted in the real world and feeling deeply inadequate in team meetings. One might say that I was humbled! Yet, in those early years because I felt vulnerable and inadequate I experienced great growth.

Upon reflection, I can say that every period of significant growth in my life has come at times when confronted with a significant challenge to accomplish something that seemed impossible. This is likely true for all of us. Our greatest growth comes when confronting something that is very difficult. The more difficult it is and the less adequate we feel, the greater the growth.

What is it about difficulty that causes growth? It is not just the fact that it is difficult but in the process of confronting the difficult thing, something happens inside of us. We feel inadequate, insecure and vulnerable. How we deal with that insecurity is what ultimately leads to personal growth. Great people, when recognizing these feelings think a little more, try a little harder, reach a little deeper, work a little longer, ask a little more often and listen a little more intently. The more anxious we feel about our inadequacy the harder, deeper, longer and more intently we approach our work. This is what causes and accelerates personal growth.

In summary, hard things create feelings of vulnerability and confronting that vulnerability with actions leads to growth. Growth based on this formula applies not to just the young, but to every single person, throughout all of our lives. We only stop growing when we either stop doing things that are hard or stop feeling inadequate or vulnerable when confronting hard things. Therefore, the foundational truth that is the reason why we lead with humility is that growth requires vulnerability. Another way to say it is, "Because growth requires vulnerability, therefore I lead with humility."

> *We only stop growing when we either stop doing things that are hard or stop feeling inadequate or vulnerable when confronting hard things.*

HUMILITY AND CONTINUOUS IMPROVEMENT

Great organizations create cultures where people are constantly confronted with very difficult challenges to which they must respond. I heard an employee in just such a company say, after only being on the job for less than three months, "They don't just want me to come to work and do my job the same way every day. They expect me to constantly be looking for a better way to do it. That is really my job. It is very hard to do but I love it. It is what makes me want to come to work every day."

When teaching these principles to executives I am often asked, "Bob, isn't it OK if I have an employee who just wants to come to work and do their job. They don't want to get involved on teams, come to meetings or do things outside of their normal work. They are loyal and dependable employees who know their jobs very well and are good at what they do. I am glad I have them. Isn't that enough?"

This is a very tough question and always invokes at least an hour of discussion. In the end most people usually conclude that, yes they are grateful for them, but ultimately that is not enough. Not only can we not just keep doing anything that we do the same way, but ultimately we are wasting all of the untapped potential of the employee. This waste is ultimately disrespectful to the person. The role of a great leader is to help every single person achieve a greater portion of his or her capabilities and experience the satisfaction that comes from personal growth. Some people need a little bit more encouragement than others but in the end, the good feelings that come from growth are innate, although perhaps buried and hidden in some.

The reason why we lead with humility is because all growth requires vulnerability and growth is what almost every leader wants to accomplish. The humility of a leader is perhaps their most visible and impactful attribute. A humble leader not only experiences great personal growth, but also empowers an entire organization for growth.

I have often heard people talk about creating a learning organization and approach it through organization structure or management systems. Only a leader who leads with humility and creates a culture where humility is valued and nurtured can ever truly create a learning organization. Learning requires growth and growth requires vulnerability. Therefore a culture where leaders lead with humility becomes a perpetual and natural learning organization.

Learning requires growth and growth requires vulnerability. Therefore a culture where leaders lead with humility becomes a perpetual and natural learning organization.

QUESTIONS NOT ANSWERS

I had a client once who engaged me to help develop the senior team to take more and more responsibility. The CEO knew that he had become the primary barrier to the growth of this group of leaders. He did this by being the Chief <u>Everything</u> Officer. No matter the question…he had the answer and try as he might, his answers always found a way of coming out. The moment this happened, group process ended and all learning and development stopped.

Leaders who lead with humility do more than just hold their answers back; they wonder what others might have to say on the topic. They listen carefully to people's comments and ask sincere questions, not to show how smart they are, or to catch the person who can't answer them, but to genuinely learn from the experience and insight of others. A leader's questions invite the person to think. The harder the question, the harder a person has to think.

Good questions from a humble leader take people out of their comfort zone and cause them to be vulnerable when they do not know the answers. Growth comes through vulnerability and successful leaders create the conditions where everyone always feels a bit vulnerable because they are always being challenged with hard questions.

Examples of some generic questions that illustrate those that might come from a humble leader include:

1. Why do you think this occurred?
2. What do you think is the best thing we could do to prevent this from happening again?
3. What do you think would make this result even better?
4. What would it take to cut the time in half or to double the outcomes?
5. What do you think we could do as a leadership team that would help you the most?

HUMILITY AND APPRECIATION

One of my favorite corporations is the OC Tanner Company located in Salt Lake City, Utah. OC Tanner employees often talk about creating a culture of appreciation, but what does it take to create a genuine culture of appreciation? Many companies have created very good recognition and reward systems but few have genuinely created a culture of appreciation. For appreciation to be sustainable in any organization, it takes far more than a cupboard full of small gifts to present to people. It takes more than a few pizza parties or a 4th of July picnic each year. A culture of appreciation is enabled and informed when leaders listen to the voice of humility and feel deeply appreciative of each associate.

Appreciation is not a system; it is a feeling and comes from the heart. Showing recognition is respectful and being respectful requires humility.

If everything has to be about me, I am never thinking about the value of others and feel no appreciation. This is what is meant in the definition of humility that says humility is not thinking less *of* yourself it is thinking less *about* yourself. The inference from this definition is that humble people think largely about others and value what they do. When a leader leads with humility they not only recognize and appreciate others but they also create opportunities for others to have the stage and share the limelight.

I know a leader who expects and supports others in doing the work but when it comes time to present it he always takes the lead and has to be seen as the leader. This is very hard not to do and it is easy to rationalize why the leader is the one who should be communicating upward or even sideways. I can think of situations over the years where I was guilty of this and missed many opportunities to recognize, reward and develop others. If I am fully honest I can see that indeed it was important to me to be recognized for the good work of others on my team. When this happened it is clear that I failed to lead with humility and an opportunity was lost. I bet I'm not alone.

IDEAL BEHAVIORS INFORMED BY THE VOICE OF THE PRINCIPLE

Leaders

1. Leaders always set aside thoughts of themselves and focus on other members of their teams.
2. Leaders openly acknowledge their mistakes and show others how they have learned from them.
3. Leaders reach down into the organization and create opportunities for people to do hard things they might not have done otherwise.

Managers

1. Managers spend time at the workplace with associates observing work, asking questions and allowing people to be accountable for answers to previously asked questions.
2. Managers are aware of the good work that others do and go out of their way to express their sincere appreciation.

3. Managers design and continuously improve great systems that make it easy for everyone to express their appreciation for others.

Associates

1. Every associate seeks out opportunities to learn new things even if they are outside of their comfort zones.
2. Associates quickly acknowledge their mistakes and ask for help when needed.
3. Associates always express appreciation to those around them for even the smallest act of kindness or support shown them.

Leading with humility is indeed an ideal behavior in and of itself. Humility is not something that comes with a brilliant flash of light and suddenly a person is humble. Certainly many can point to some traumatic event in their life that was life changing. For most of us however, the attitude and mindset of humility is developed over many years, through hundreds if not thousands of small life experiences and often under the watchful tutelage of a caring and wise coach.

As Jims Collins has stated, a leader who has listened to the voice of humility possesses a duality of attributes; they are "modest and willful, shy and fearless." Being humble does not require one to be weak, introverted or non-confrontational. On the contrary it takes great courage to trust that others will elevate themselves to the high expectations given them. It takes wisdom to ask questions and coach rather than simply direct the work of others and it takes self-confidence to allow others to get the recognition for achievement.

I once saw a sign on a great leader's desk that read, "There is no limit to what a man (or woman) can achieve if they do not care who gets the recognition." This greatness is what comes from listening to the voice of the powerful and enabling principle of *Leading with Humility*.

7

Seek Perfection

The goal must be to permanently embed the mindset and skills of continuous improvement deeper into every element of every organization in every industry and make them sustainable over the long term.

CONTINUOUS IMPROVEMENT

For those of you with experience in what is often called "Continuous Improvement" this chapter and the next few will have a familiar ring. For readers not yet exposed to Lean, Total Quality Management, Just-in-Time, Six Sigma, etc. do not fear. This may actually be easier for you in that you have less to unlearn and may be more open to hear the voice of the five principles covered in these four chapters and are less likely to get hooked on the tools associated with them.

It helps to think of continuous improvement as a mindset rather than a program. This chapter will describe the first of five key guiding principles that have been at the root of continuous improvement initiatives for over 50 years. When our team at the Shingo Institute began our research we first had to know why programs of continuous improvement were not sustainable or continuous. We identified five key reasons and knew that for the Shingo Prize to remain viable and more importantly, to lead the way, our work had to address all of them. Key reasons were:

1. That senior management had not yet found their proper role in the overall initiatives, therefore tended to disengage.

2. That the programs were seen as just that, important but a separate thing from the strategic business of providing goods and services to customers.
3. That responsibility for running the programs was usually delegated down into the organization often with a separate organization set up to run them.
4. That implementation of the programs almost always migrated toward training and the application of tools to identify and solve problems.
5. That because they were seen as programs they were viewed by top management as having a beginning and an end. One good idea with its associated program was successively replaced with the next greatest idea with its associated tools and program.

Make no mistake; these programs of continuous improvement have resulted in innumerable great results. Cumulatively, hundreds of millions of dollars have been saved and millions of customers better served by the improvements created as a consequence of these new tools and the people who have learned to use them.

The goal of our research was to determine how to help people more permanently embed these great practices deeper into the organization, make them sustainable over the long term and expand their application into every element of every organization in every industry.

Once we came to understand that for the mindset of continuous improvement to be sustainable it had to be embedded into the culture, we had to determine what to ground culture in. As discussed in Chapter One, for culture to be sustainable it cannot be based on management fads, the personality of an individual leader or values that change over time. Sustainable cultures of excellence must be deeply grounded in the bedrock principles of "operational excellence." Note that for this chapter I used the phrase Operational Excellence rather than Enterprise Excellence. This is only because in this case the principles to be discussed below are almost entirely about the way in which we execute our strategies. By now we understand that the voice of the two principles of *Respect for Every Individual* and *Lead with Humility* are the enablers for everything else, especially the creation of operational or execution excellence.

The five principles whose voices we will learn to hear are:

1. Seek Perfection
2. Assure Quality at the Source

3. Flow (and Pull) Value
4. Embrace Scientific Thinking
5. Focus on Process

Note that each of these five principles is again stated in the form of an action. They each possess both a verb and a noun; **Seek** perfection, **Assure** Quality at the Source, **Focus** on Process, **Flow** (and **Pull**) Value and **Embrace** Scientific Thinking. Principles govern outcomes and are grounded in foundational truths, which make them universal and timeless.

Principles govern outcomes and are grounded in foundational truths, which make them universal and timeless.

THE VOICE OF THE PRINCIPLE ... *SEEK PERFECTION*

Of the five principles this one is the most foundational. The principle of *Seek Perfection* describes a mindset and a commitment to live with a never-ending dissatisfaction with things the way they are and a powerful drive to constantly be seeking a better way. When this mindset has been built into a culture the hardest part is done. The voices of the remaining four principles provide an outline for where to look and how to satisfy a burning passion for continuous improvement (*Seek Perfection*).

I once worked with a man who by any standard people would describe as a perfectionist. I loved this man and working very closely with him for nearly ten years had a profound impact on my own standards of what "a job well done" should be. There is no doubt that what I once esteemed to be "good enough" raised several notches during those years.

Along with his many great qualities, I also observed the problems associated with almost compulsive expectations of every single person for every single detail. We all grew but we all experienced the unintended negative consequences of a penchant for being overly pedantic. This is not what is meant by the principle of *Seek Perfection*.

The voice of this principle does not expect perfection in everything but rather the emphasis is in the **seeking**. Perfection is the target on the horizon. Personal growth and organizational continuous improvement are the products of a relentless pursuit or search for it.

RELENTLESSLY SEEKING

We will talk in chapter ten about Scientific Thinking and discuss a model for continuous improvement developed in conjunction with development of the Toyota system of management shortly after the Second World War. This system for continuous improvement is called the Deming wheel (Figure 7.1) and is sometimes also referred to as the Shewhart cycle. Both Deming and Shewhart were early pioneers in development of the tools associated with continuous improvement. The wheel or cycle took on a hundred variations of the following basic image.

The wheel also became known as the PDCA wheel after the four basic steps in the process, namely Plan, Do, Check and finally Act. Later versions of the wheel changed the A from Act to Adjust; Plan, Do, Check, Adjust. In reality this change is largely symbolic because the vast majority of people and organizations never get past the PD steps. Plan Do, Plan Do and Plan Do, or even worse Do, Do, Do; or Plan, Plan, Plan! With so many problems to solve the most that usually gets done is the Plan Do then on to the next burning platform. The outcome of this default approach to continuous improvement is that problems get addressed mostly at the symptom level. Far too often solutions do not address the root cause of problems and rarely is there a check and adjust element to the effort, that is until they become big enough problems again.

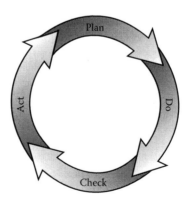

FIGURE 7.1
PDCA, or Deming wheel. (From Deming, W. E., *Out of the Crisis.* Cambridge, MA: Massachusetts Institute of Technology, Center for Advanced Engineering Study, 1986.)

Far too often solutions do not address the root cause and rarely is there a check and adjust element to the effort, that is until they become big enough problems again.

A culture that is able to hear the voice of the principle of *Seek Perfection* would never be content to simply institute a change and then move on. All of us have experienced far too often the frustrating experience of solving the same problem over and over again. Usually they take on a slightly different appearance but at the root, they are simply different manifestations of the same problem.

De facto cultures almost always gravitate to this state and call it a culture of fire fighting. Fix a problem well enough to keep going and then go on to the next fire, only to come back when the first one flares up again. No one likes this culture except perhaps the arsonists who are continually hailed as heroes for putting out the most fires.

The only way to solve this problem once and for all is to create a culture of *Seek Perfection*. If you are seeking perfection you take the time required to be certain you are fixing the right thing, at the right place and with the right people. A fundamental part of this culture must be an extremely disciplined system to continuously monitor the solution (C – check, in the PDCA cycle) and constantly be seeking even better ways to fix the problem (A – adjust, in the PDCA cycle). Ultimately the voice of the principle instructs us to eliminate any possibility that it could ever happen again; this is called a fail-safe and is in fact a form of perfection.

The voice of the principle does guide the creation of these kinds of systems but most importantly the principle informs our thinking, beliefs and ultimately our values. If we value heroic fire fighters more than quiet individuals and teams that one small improvement at a time just keep making things better and better, you will always have fires and fire fighters. If we value never-ending continuous improvement by every single person, every single day in every single part of the organization, we will eventually clear out the underbrush and debris such that no fuel remains from which a fire can start. This is another way to describe perfection.

If we value never-ending continuous improvement by every single person, every single day in every single part of the organization, we will eventually clear out the underbrush and debris such that no fuel remains from which a fire can start.

FULL PARTICIPATION

Creating a culture where everyone has the mindset of seeking perfection requires also the full participation of every single person in the organization. *Respect for Every Individual* and *Leading with Humility* are the most powerful enablers of a culture where seeking perfection can thrive. The number of problems to be solved at every level of every organization is so great that there is no way for a few experts or thinkers or professionals or staffers or managers to solve all of them as fast as they occur.

Seeking Perfection requires all hands on deck. Failure to get all hands on deck can come about from either a lack of humility or by simply allowing the de facto culture to emerge. Deferring problem solving to managers, staffers and experts is the easiest, simplest and fastest thing to do, but by definition also has the greatest number of limitations, namely the size of the pool of problem solvers. A leader who is listening to the voice of this principle invests in the development of every single person to become part of this critical and continuously improving army of problem solvers. There is no doubt it is an investment but the payback in both tangible and intangible benefits should make the case for investing an easy decision. The will, leadership and competency to gain full participation are most often the constraints. The voice of the principle literally shouts the need to act.

I have a very good friend who is the CEO of a very successful privately held firm. My friend is a wonderful human being with a great love for the people. He often talks about what it means to him to have gone for well over 20 years without having a single layoff, all the while growing the business into a very large multi-national corporation. He is one of the few CEOs who has personally gotten involved in not only the tools but also the processes that might support continuous improvement. In spite of the numerous great things that have happened in his company, he remained disappointed in the rate of improvement and the determination of many systemic problems to remain unsolved.

After several sessions with his senior management team and multiple visits to their *Gemba* what became clear is that only a relatively small percentage of the workforce were actually involved daily in solving chronic problems. The "few" who were, were frantically trying to fix things but the rate that new problems surfaced often seemed to exceed the rate at which the "few" could fix them. The CEO was finally able to see this when we were studying the principle of *Seek Perfection*. He had boundless stories to share of the few who were using great tools to continuously make things better but finally admitted that continuous improvement was not really a part of the culture of the entire organization.

A few people were frantically trying to fix things but the rate at which new problems surfaced often seemed to exceed the rate at which the "few" could actually fix them.

The more he thought about it, the more disappointed he became in himself for not being the kind of leader who trusted and empowered every employee with the expectation that they also become involved in daily continuous improvement. For him it was not a question of will, it was a question of awareness and skill. It was the voice of the principle that revealed to him a critical part of his own leadership that was missing.

THE POSSIBILITY OF PERFECTION

A word about perfection. This debate occurs routinely, "But is perfection really possible?" Most people say no and in general I agree with them. But perfection is technically possible and really depends on how you define it, which is why the "Seeking" part of the principle is so important.

To illustrate how perfection is technically possible I offer this example. Perfection really depends on the standard or the target. When people set a target for improvement and measure themselves as they improve, once they get to and consistently surpass the target one could say that they have become perfect in that thing. Are they perfect? No, but they are perfect in their ability to hit that target every time.

People who hear the voice of this principle set stretch goals then celebrate when they become perfect at achieving them. Almost immediately, they then set new and higher goals that reveal entirely new problems to solve. These are problems that are not visible when the standard was lower. Only by continuously raising the bar do more and more of the rocks become exposed. With all hands on deck and a mindset of *Seeking Perfection* in achievement of the new and higher goal, the individual or team begin solving the new problems one at a time until little by little they become perfect in that new thing. This then is a cause for celebration, and of course raising the bar and setting an even higher standard.

Some might say, "Isn't that depressing to people, to keep raising the bar? Don't they begin to feel like they can never win, or no matter what they do it's never good enough?" This critical question can only be answered by understanding the foundational truth that sits below the principle and gives it voice.

FOUNDATIONAL TRUTH ONE ... *SEEK PERFECTION*

The desire to improve is innate to every human being.

I came to understand the foundational truth below this principle by watching my father while I was growing up. My dad loved his garden and his flowerbeds and of course that meant that his children either learned to love them also or they were miserable for having to work in them every year. Every year I wondered why he couldn't just leave things alone. No sooner did we get the beds looking great, than he had some new idea about how to make them even better. He never seemed to stop. Year after year he made continuous improvements to both the appearance of his flower garden and the productivity of his vegetable garden. At the end of a long hot summer day I vividly remember watching him walk around the entire house and through his garden with a warm smile on his face as he took in the most recent improvements we had made.

Little by little I came to see the work not as a burden but as an opportunity to feel the joy of having made something better. As an adult I now find myself doing exactly the same thing. I mow my lawn two and sometimes three directions always trying to find the best cut. I experiment with new fertilizers and weed treatments always trying to find ways to get more satisfaction in the evenings from sitting on the patio and looking at the perfectly straight mow lines and the weed-less dark green lawn.

Perhaps not in lawn and garden details but in a thousand other ways people of all walks of life find joy and satisfaction out of making improvements in their lives. Improvements in their work and in their standard of living, improvements in their homes and living conditions, improvements in the practice of their hobbies, improvements in the lives of their children and grandchildren. Even small improvements bring satisfaction to everyone. Politicians speak of the economy and their efforts to make people's lives better.

Most people become dissatisfied and discontent when anything becomes static. Improvement and progress is the fuel that feeds the soul. My wife, watching me work very hard to improve the quality of outcomes from my business has often said, worried no doubt about strain on me, "Why do you always have to keep growing the business? Why isn't it good enough to just leave it the way it is?" For many years I answered her with a discussion about competition, changing markets and growing demands on our financial resources. In recent years I have come to see this very differently.

Improvement and progress is the fuel that feeds the soul.

Although the reasons I used to give were valid, I now know that the real driver for my need to continuously improve is less about external factors and more about internal factors. Something inside of me needs to be a part of making things better. When I stop growing I start to die. I know that if left to die for too long the toll on my spirit and eventually my body would become irreparable.

I believe that this natural law is true not just for me but for everyone. Evidence of this transformation can be seen in the often-rapid decline in mental and physical health of a person after they retire from a life of hard work and accomplishments.

My father, who is also fiercely independent, is now 97 years old. Two years ago I helped him refinish his deck, he found it impossible to just watch me work. He had to be down on his hands and knees sanding and applying stain. A year later he still comments on how great the deck looks and in what year we will need to do it again. Even at 97 improvement still feeds his soul.

FOUNDATIONAL TRUTH TWO ... *SEEK PERFECTION*

Our ability to improve is only limited by our expectations and paradigms.

Have you ever heard someone say after doing something amazing, "I didn't think I would ever be able to do that!" Of course we have. Every day people achieve amazing things they never thought possible; nevertheless they do them and often even more. A significant constraint in achieving greatness or continuous improvement or perfection in a specific thing is the often self-imposed limit that we place on ourselves. Joel Barker often talks about these things as paradigms, or the rules that govern our ability to see anything else (Barker 1993).

Seeking Perfection requires a continual reshaping of our internal sense of what is possible. When great leaders hear the voice of this principle, they actively seek opportunities for everyone to expand their view of what is possible. This happens through challenging assignments, great questions, being accountable, good measurements, education, mentoring and just being around others who are constantly doing amazing and breakthrough things. Good visual management systems help people to see constraints and observe their elimination, giving hope and faith in future achievement.

By combining both elements of this foundational truth into a single statement we can conclude that: the desire to continuously improve is innate to every human being and that our ability to improve is only limited by our expectations and paradigms.

This statement is a natural law or said conversely, it is a law of nature. It is true now, it has always been true and it will be true in a thousand years, in a hundred years and certainly through the current planning period. It is the reason why we *Seek Perfection*. Inside of every one of our employees there is a fire, sometimes small and sometimes raging. A great leader who hears the voice of this principle creates a culture that daily fuels and fans the flame of continuous improvement that burns inside each of us. In the end, improvement will be what people primarily work for. It will be the thing that causes every associate and colleague at the end of the day to take one last walk around his or her area of work and smile with deep personal satisfaction at the improvements they made that day.

A great leader who hears the voice of this principle creates a culture that daily fuels and fans the flame of continuous improvement that burns inside each of us.

Near the end of the Shingo Institute's course they call Discover Excellence, there is a quote from Mr. Eiji Toyoda, former President and Chairman of Toyota Motor Corporation. He said, "…employees are offering a very important part of their lives to us. If we don't use their time effectively, we are wasting their lives." This is the voice of the principle *Seek Perfection* speaking to every leader and manager. Respect every individual enough to allow them to act on their innate desire to make things better and make a difference and help them to create new personal paradigms for what is possible in their work and lives.

People who are deeply grounded in this principle have a perpetual discontent with the way things are. They always see what is possible and aspire to improve. A principle that is understood and accepted becomes a continuous voice speaking in our heads and in our hearts reminding us that there is always much more that can be done; the clearer the voice, the greater the motivation to improve. Listening to the principles invokes and almost ensures a mindset of humility and continuous improvement.

A principle that is understood and accepted becomes a continuous voice speaking in our heads and in our hearts reminding us that there is always much more that can be done; the clearer the voice, the greater the motivation to improve.

Great leaders creating cultures of excellence never stop communicating the voice of this principle every day and to every person.

8

Assure Quality at the Source

The establishment of stretch goals is ultimately not a management process, it is the natural outcome of people who see beyond the mark and are motivated by the voice of principles.

THE VOICE OF THE PRINCIPLE ...
ASSURE QUALITY AT THE SOURCE

When I graduated from university in 1976 I went to work for John Deere. I had never been in a factory the size of their Harvester Works facility and was dazzled every time I had an opportunity to leave my office and visit the final assembly line. When the glitz finally wore off I began to notice things more closely and as they really were. In front of every assembly station were large totes of parts waiting to be used on the line. Most parts had been made far away in some remote location, by people who knew very little about where the parts they made were used or the impact their work had on others. Some parts had been made weeks if not months earlier and usually in very large quantities called Economic Order Quantities or EOQ's.

The factory was located on a large property near the edge of the Mississippi River. Out the back door of the factory was a very large holding area where the (mostly finished) combines that could not be shipped for one reason or another waited for repairs. The first time I stepped out the door and saw the sea of green I remember being both shocked and amazed. Several large teams of highly skilled employees moved like ants through the combines trying to identify all of their problems and find solutions.

In each case they produced a unique list of the problems created by someone far upstream that did not become visible until it was too late. The combines were on a moving chain and could not be removed. The only option was to finish the combine around the problem and then fix it later, always at great cost to the customer and the company.

This was over 40 years ago and of course the brilliant employees at Deere and Co. have long since solved these problems, but I saw a version of the same problem at a car manufacturing company very recently. As a new product came down the final assembly line, cars were pulled off that could not be completed for one reason or another. With no place to put them, these cars were parked anywhere they could find a spot. New scratches and broken side mirrors from the process added to the post production line repairs. In the end, the cars were beautiful but the cost of this process was staggering.

Most of us are a part of some larger system and almost everything we do impacts and is impacted by others in some way.

Most of us are a part of some larger system and almost everything we do impacts others in some way. This is true in almost every element of any enterprise. It is true in banks, insurance companies, hospitals, stores as well as factories. Every mistake that requires someone else to fix it later adds waste in the form of time and cost, and shows disrespect for those who must fix them. In some enterprises, a single mistake may jeopardize the health or even the life of another person. All mistakes have a consequence; the difference is only a matter of degree.

All mistakes have a consequence; the difference is only a matter of degree.

To solve the problem of allowing defects or mistakes to get passed forward, every person must become accountable for the accuracy of everything they do. This principle is called *Assure Quality at the Source* and listening to and acting on the voice of this principle will fundamentally transform almost every metric of any organization.

When a culture is designed to *Assure Quality at the Source* people never allow anything they are responsible for to be passed forward to someone else until they know for certain that it is right. Every situation dictates a different set of solutions in order to assure quality but cultures of excellence spend a great deal of their resources to make sure it can happen. Tools, training, time, information, equipment and standards are only a few examples of what must be aligned so that people can be accountable for the quality of what they do.

It is a foundational truth that it is in the nature of all human beings to want to do things right.

THE VOICE OF THE PRINCIPLE ... *FOCUS ON THE PROCESS*

When a mistake does get made, rather than immediately blaming the person, leaders first ask, "What about this process is not working that would allow this mistake to occur?" Notice that the focus is not on who is wrong but what is wrong. The principle is described as *Focus on the Process. A foundational truth behind this principle is that all outcomes are a consequence of a process.* Even a good person in a bad process will usually fail, eventually. An average person in a brilliant process has a very good chance of being successful and will eventually make the process even better. Great people come from great processes.

In order for a person to be able to *Assure Quality at the Source,* they must have excellent processes. Great processes are not created perfect the first time; rather, little by little, one small idea at a time, processes get better and better *(Seek Perfection)* and more able to *Assure Quality at the Source* the first time.

A good person in a bad process will usually fail, eventually. An average person in a brilliant process has a very good chance of being successful and will eventually make the process even better.

This then becomes a key responsibility of frontline managers, to continuously improve the systems and work processes being used by people every day in the course of doing their work. The number of problems that must be solved to assure quality at the source of every person's work is so large that typically it requires the expertise and commitment of every single person in the organization *(Respect for Every Individual* and *Think Systemically).*

To show respect for the people doing the work, owners of the work should be considered the "experts" and placed in a central, if not leadership role in conceiving and implementing needed process improvements. These principles speak, "Everyone, every day, everywhere."

PULL THE CHAIN AND FIX THE PROCESS

It takes great courage and integrity for leaders and managers to embrace the principle of *Assuring Quality at the Source*. When an employee says, "Something is wrong," a leader must be prepared to stop the workflow until the root cause can be determined and a solution put into place. The first time you decide you can't afford to stop, it's all over. We often figuratively call this, "Pulling the Chain." On a moving assembly line, workers often have a chain, or rope or cord that is available to workers just in case something happens that they cannot overcome while the line is passing through their station. When they pull the chain, the whole line stops and dozens of people are unable to continue working. The cardinal rule is that until the problem is solved the line cannot start up again. These are the moments of truth for leaders when they demonstrate to everyone else that they really do believe in the principle.

Every organization that has a culture of *Assuring Quality at the Source* will find numerous places and times when every employee must figuratively "pull the chain."

CELEBRATE PROBLEMS TO FIX THE PROCESS

A number of years ago I took a group of executives to visit factories in Japan. After five amazing days the entire group of 18 senior executives from many different countries and industries unanimously agreed the thing that surprised them the most was what one company called a "mistake board." The board was just the tool but what was amazing was the culture this company had where mistakes were celebrated. Rather than creating a culture where mistakes get buried, they built a culture where having the courage to acknowledge a mistake as soon as it happens was celebrated.

Of course along with the philosophy and the tool, meaning the board, they had an entire system for also identifying if the person knew how it happened, what the solution was to prevent it from happening again and had the solution been implemented. All of this information was put on the most visible wall in the facility along with a picture of the smiling person who had made the mistake. (For most of us this seems like an oxymoron.)

It then became the responsibility of every other person in the company to look at the board every day and if something showed up that they knew something about, they were to immediately offer their assistance in solving the problem. Mistake makers and problem solvers came from everywhere in the business at all levels.

Think of the difference between this culture and most others you have experienced. The leaders of this Japanese company clearly demonstrated a culture of *Respect for Every Individual, Leading with Humility, Seek Perfection, Assure Quality at the Source* and *Focus on Process*. These were not just slogans or boards on the wall but deeply held convictions about the behaviors that ultimately maximize value creation for customers and profitability for shareholders.

INCREASE THE NUMBER OF PROBLEMS TO FIX THE PROCESS

In another business I was in I met with a team that was responsible for launching a new product line. This was a very complex product that had essentially never been made before with a lot of startup costs. Before the issues were even identified, someone found a buyer for a significant number of the products if they could be produced almost immediately at a certain volume and at a certain price. A deal was signed and a new team went to work. (Sound familiar?)

Soon they had the line up and running but to their horror, after all they could think to do they were only able to produce less than half of the contracted parts per day and at significantly more cost than required. One morning when the team was huddling before the shift started they were talking about the problems they had solved but also about the enormous number of problems yet to be solved most of which they hadn't even seen yet. One employee said something like, "I bet I can solve more problems than you!" and immediately it became a competition. A goal was created by the team to identify and solve problems, the more, the better.

A visual system for tracking problems and ensuring their resolution was created. The visual display of their commitment to an aggressive goal required them to be accountable to each other, the company and most importantly to the customer.

Over the course of several months this team went from as few as five or six problems a week identified to nearly a hundred problems per day either solved or identified with action items for resolution. Each time they reached a new high they had a quick celebration, raised the bar and then immediately went back to work solving more problems. Managers, supervisors, lead operators, operators, maintenance personnel and engineers all became a part of the competition and this corps of problem solvers. They proudly called themselves master problem solvers and had built a unique and powerful culture based on all of the principles we have been describing.

THE VALUE OF A STANDARD IN PROBLEM SOLVING

Shigeo Shingo used to say… "No problem…BIG problem!" He taught that the first ingredient in recognizing a problem is to have a standard. In the absence of a standard, there can be no defect. People with no standard have no way of knowing whether they are succeeding or failing, getting better or getting worse or winning or losing. I have often heard this described as playing competitive basketball without a scoreboard. Great leaders never let their teams work without a standard. It is not just poor management; it is disrespectful.

> *Great leaders never let their teams work without a standard. It is not just poor management; it is disrespectful.*

One surefire way of knowing whether or not a team has a standard is to ask people what problems they have or how they could make their work better. If they are hesitant and struggle to come up with anything significant, you can bet they do not have a standard or a leader who is helping them to see and focus on a visible gap.

A standard becomes a target or aspiration and can be created in many ways. A goal, written down, agreed to and made visible can become a standard. A specification that defines the quality criteria can become a standard and the voice of a principle can also define a standard.

Listening to and hearing the voice of principles creates in everyone an entirely new and immensely high standard. A principle in fact speaks to the ultimate standard. In Shingo speak we often called this an "ideal." Since quality is measured as performance to a standard, clarity of what the standard is, is essential for ownership and accountability. The clearer the voice of the principle becomes the higher people raise the bar.

This truth is I believe one of the most important reasons why everyone in every organization must understand principles. The establishment of stretch goals is ultimately not a management process, it is the natural outcome of people who see beyond the mark and are motivated by the voice of principles.

> *The establishment of stretch goals is ultimately not a management process, it is the natural outcome of people who see beyond the mark and are motivated by the voice of principles.*

UNSOLVED PROBLEMS AND THE HUMAN SPIRIT

In the previous chapter I mentioned a culture of fire fighting. One of the most common sources of waste and frustration in almost every organization comes from failing to hear the principle of *Assuring Quality at the Source*. In order to assure quality, problems must be solved in a way that they do not and in fact cannot reoccur, hence the word "assure."

The value of solving problems once and for all is universal. It applies in banks, hospitals, retail stores, construction sites, and offices and flows from the principle of *Assuring Quality at the Source*. Think of the waste associated with continuing to experience the same known problem over and over again. This waste manifests itself in countless ways but perhaps the most impactful is damage to the human spirit when it appears to employees that no one really cares.

The further down the organization a problem is manifested, the greater the probability that resolution requires the help of others. When employees care enough to wave the flag identifying the issue but no one comes, or they come but don't act, the consequence is devastating. Even good people eventually take on the attitude that, "If they don't care, why should I." Imagine the loss to an organization when people get to that spot. What is lost includes not only their current capabilities but also all of their untapped potential. When this happens we waste people's lives.

To prevent this travesty, leaders should make certain that the principle of *Assuring Quality at the Source* is deeply understood and committed to by everyone, beginning especially with senior management. In the case of leaders, commitment means that they be present at the *Gemba* and possess the humility to ask employees how the management team is doing at supporting the resolution of known issues.

IDEAL BEHAVIORS

Leaders should make certain that very strong systems are in place to encourage both problems and ideas for their resolution to come forward and then get acted on as quickly as is possible. Leaders must be prepared to make hard decisions that are usually associated with chronic problems. There is usually a reason why chronic problems are chronic. To *Assure Quality at the Source*, these are the root problems that must be solved.

Manager's ideal behaviors would be demonstrated in the way they solicit the participation of employees to identify and solve the problems. Managers can create powerful visual management systems that assure associates they have been heard and that the problems they experience are being addressed. Perhaps most importantly, managers can find ways to involve both the people where the problem originates and the people most affected by the problem in its solution. Managers create opportunities for people to go home at night full of enthusiasm for what they did at work that really made a difference. Solving reoccurring problems that waste people's lives really makes a difference. This all comes from hearing the voice of the principle that speaks of *Assuring Quality at the Source*.

You have probably noticed by now that principles rarely sing solos. Recognizing the impact of a principle almost always points to other principles as well, especially in solving the problems required to assure quality. Being able to hear principles together is almost like hearing a quartet of beautiful voices or maybe even a quintet. To assure quality at the source, many principles must be combined.

9

Flow Value to Customers

Everything flows; it is only a question of at what rate.

THE VOICE OF THE PRINCIPLE ...
FLOW VALUE TO CUSTOMERS

Near my home runs a river called the Blacksmith Fork. A favorite place to ride my horse is along an escarpment that overlooks the river. I love to sit in the saddle and watch the water roll over the endless number of rocks at the river's bottom. Every place the water hits a rock, it deviates from its natural course and temporarily goes a different direction. Each time it changes course, it collides with water trying to get around a different rock. The overall effect of this enormously tumultuous cascade of frustrated water is grand to watch but almost impossible to tame into anything useful.

Most of our businesses are much like the Blacksmith Fork River. Rocks of every imaginable size and shape are constantly interrupting the natural course of work from so many good people. Each rock requires a pause in the creation of value and redirection of effort long enough to get around the barrier. Each time that work deviates from its natural flow, it bumps into someone else's work and causes it to deviate as well, and on and on throughout the entire enterprise. From the employees' perspective these constant disruptions are frustrating, discouraging and eventually demoralizing. Unlike my view of the river from the escarpment that was grand, the view of your organization from the customer's perspective may appear chaotic, disorganized, unprofessional, disappointing and perhaps even underserving of their trust.

Now picture a river flowing with a perfectly sandy bottom and smooth shores all along its path. No ripples and not a single deviation. I recently sailed on a river just such as this in Ireland, the Shannon. At times along this beautiful and historic river I became completely disoriented because even though the current was actually quite strong, because of the lack of ripples I often could not tell which way the water was flowing.

This metaphor creates the framework through which we can discuss the principle of *Flowing Value*. I often tell leaders that in every organization everything flows. Information flows, ideas flow, decisions flow, money flows, projects flow, orders flow, work flows; it is only a question of at what rate is it flowing. A well-balanced scorecard should always include a measurement of the rate of flow.

This principle is based on the foundational truth that anything that disrupts the continuous creation of value is waste. Eliminating barriers to flow maximizes value creation. Maximizing the output of a stream of anything is best done by identifying and eliminating everything that gets in its way, no matter how small.

This principle is based on the foundational truth that anything that disrupts the continuous creation of value is waste.

I remember once standing at a water faucet that generated a perfect column of water. This column did not have a single ripple or even a single bubble in it. It was a perfect example of uninterrupted flow. What if all of our businesses operated just the same way, not a single cause for value to be disrupted from its course toward the customer?

As I stood at the sink in the men's room reflecting, I suspect I became somewhat of a spectacle. Especially when I discovered that the closer I placed my finger to the stream that the static electricity discharged between my finger and the water column actually caused it to become distorted along the edge. I had introduced waste into the stream.

This principle is incredibly important to any enterprise. Anything, no matter how small, that disrupts the continuous flow of value creates waste in the organization. The voice of this principle is very easy for everyone to hear. Everyone when asked, "What are all of the things that prevent you from getting your job done?" can come up with a list, sometimes a very long list. What you really asked was, "What are all of the things that interrupt or impede in any way the continuous flow of value through your area?" This is a great way to start engaging employees in the continuous improvement efforts of the organization. While you are working together to resolve the barriers, teach them all about the principle of flow.

VALUE STREAMS

Value, the thing that customers are willing to pay for, should flow continuously through the organization. The path that value takes is often referred to as a "value stream." One of the often-used tools for business improvement is called a "value stream map" or VSM. A VSM documents this flow of value through the enterprise, identifying all the specific work done at each step in the process as what the customer wants becomes progressively more valuable to them.

A value stream map becomes a visual representation of the way work gets done and makes visible for people which of the steps add value and which represent "rocks" or waste in the stream. Rocks, or barriers to the continuous flow of value, become problems to be solved and requires the engagement of everyone who can help.

To help people see how this applies to them, try using the following simple outline.

1. Ask people to identify what component of customer value they contribute.
2. Then ask them how to describe and document how that value flows through their area.
3. Finally ask people to describe all of the barriers to the flow of that value.

Rocks, or barriers to the continuous flow of value, become problems to be solved and require the engagement of everyone who can help.

For example if the person worked in the accounting department, they might describe the customer value component they contribute as an accurate and timely invoice. To accomplish this, the information required might flow through eight separate steps involving six different people, four email transactions, seven computer screens, four decisions and ten days. All of this would be documented in a way that illustrates not only the flow, but also the rate of flow over time. Added to the value stream map might be the points in the process that are most problematic, take the most time, create the most rework or are the hardest to accomplish. This information might then become the target of a year-long employee led effort to eliminate each of the actions that are barriers to a continuous flow of timely and error-free invoices. Don't forget that the more problems you solve, the more problems you can see.

Remember the metaphor of the static electricity disrupting the flow of water? When employees focus on increasing the rate of flow it will most likely not come from one or two big ideas, but rather from hundreds of small or even very small improvements that add up. I took some executives to a company in Japan that tells their employees that if they can save either a penny or a second, they should make the change. Their goal was to create a culture of continuous improvement where everyone, everywhere and every day is identifying the problems that impede the continuous flow of value to customers. They know that not only do the little things add up but mixed in with the little ideas will come a few very large ideas that will become transformational.

PULL VALUE

In the Shingo Model and elsewhere you will often see along with the principle of *Flow Value* the companion concept of *Pull Value*. To illustrate this concept imagine again the water faucet. When you want the water, you open the spigot and water flows. When you do not want the water, you leave it closed and you get no water. It's as simple as that. If water flows, like it did in my daughter's home when she was sleeping and the washing machine got stuck in the fill cycle, what is flowing is of no value; in fact it is waste.

Product that flows without demand is pure waste. This was the part of the old EOQ (Economic Order Quantity) model that did not work. Value in that case is not measured in terms of what customers want and are willing to pay for if they knew they were being charged for it; it is being measured in terms of some other internal efficiency factor. The list of unwanted outcomes from producing ahead of actual demand is very, very long. Yet, the perceived need to do so is real when a business is operating out of a certain paradigm.

Beginning the value creation process based only on real demand (Pull) is not easy, it requires many years of problem identification and solving at virtually every level and in almost every function of the enterprise. In fact it requires a complete remake of the business paradigms that drive virtually every facet of work. Purchasing and supplier relationships must change, machine design and plant layout needs to change, inventory policies need to change and every barrier that impedes the continuous flow of value must be identified and eliminated. Even marketing, sales and distribution strategies and paradigms must change, and perhaps most importantly, first time quality at every source must be assured. Every single employee from leaders to managers to frontline associates must become involved in identifying the hundreds and even thousands of details that must be executed to flow value to customers based only on real demand (Pull). This transformational principle of *the continuous flow of value to customers* can become a long-term vision or a key strategic objective under which many supportive strategies, goals, and initiatives may be organized.

FLOW AND JOB SATISFACTION

The same things that create waste and impede flow are often the very things that employees dislike the most about their work or are the least safe. Imagine how exciting it would be for an employee if their manager asked them to identify every element of work that is frustrating, unsafe or clearly adds no value, and consider ways that each of them might be eliminated. This manager just might become leading candidate for the "manager of the year" award.

The team's "idea board" would almost immediately be filled with opportunities for improvement. The principle of *Flowing Value* to customers becomes the voice that reveals gaps between current realities and a much higher standard of excellence, *continuous flow*. The interesting thing is that people understand this principle immediately and are eager to share both current and untapped skills to solve the many problems they clearly have a stake in. Once barriers to the flow of value start to diminish, improvement can be measured in the "rate of flow." The goal is always to increase the rate at which value flows to customers.

This kind of thinking is how the team of Master Problem Solvers was able to identify so many problems that were barriers to increasing the rate of product flow and eliminate the costs that customers were unwilling to pay for.

REMEMBER THE PRINCIPLE

Until a principle becomes a natural part of who people are and how they think, leaders must continue to give a voice to each and every principle. I recently had an experience while visiting a great company that had received the Shingo Prize several years ago. As we walked through their facility the President and Vice President of Operations were proud to show my client and me all of the wonderful things they continued to do since receiving the Prize. With very little encouragement employees all along our route eagerly shared what they were doing and talked about their great culture.

Both of the senior leaders had a great deal to say about *Respecting Every Single Person, Leading with Humility* and *Seeking Perfection.* While we were stopped at one location, I noticed that the Ops VP became distracted and was somewhat animated in a conversation he was having with an engineer in the final stages of starting up a new and very expensive machine.

When we were ready to move on he came up to me and said, "Bob, I am so glad you came here today. You reminded me that all of the principles are important and we totally forgot to think about the principle of *Flowing Value* when we designed and placed this machine into production." He then went on to describe four or five key things that he had just then seen that they didn't even think of. Thinking about the principle had suddenly made it clear that the way they had designed and implemented their new machine would be less valuable in achieving their overall vision than they had hoped. Some of the issues he described might be mitigated but others were now baked into the hardware. It only took five minutes for these omissions to become visible when viewed through the voice of the principle of *Flowing Value.*

Every project should begin with an analysis of each key principle of Enterprise Excellence and how that project will respond to the voice of the principles.

The actual consideration of principles is far easier to do than remembering to do it. Every project should begin with an analysis of each key principle of Enterprise Excellence and address how that project, whatever it is, will respond to and amplify the voice of the principles. The responsibility to make sure this is happening lies with the senior leadership team; it is a part of their 80%. Good design of strategic and tactical planning as well as well conceived capital appropriation systems might have mitigated the post-project revelation described above.

The actual consideration of principles is far easier to do than remembering to do it.

THE VOICE OF THE PRINCIPLE ...
CREATE VALUE FOR CUSTOMERS

This principle actually is found under the heading in the Shingo model of Results because measurements of results through any lens other than through the lens of the customer is myopic. Customers are the reason we come to work and have businesses at all. Were it not for customers, most of our organizations would cease to exist. Just as *Respect for Every Individual* sits at the foundation of the Shingo pyramid of principles because it is the greatest enabler of a culture of excellence, *Create Value for Customers* sits at the top because it answers the ultimate question of *why.*

I have a client who is very altruistic about his business. The older he gets, the more he sees the purpose of the business as a place that enables the improvement of lives. I love him for these thoughts but none of that is possible without a continuous focus on value creation for his customers. Failing that, his company will be of little value to anyone.

Value is the thing that customers want so much that they are willing to pay you to receive it. They came to you largely because they feel this is where they will receive the greatest value for their investment. With very few exceptions, the minute a customer feels they no longer receive the value they are paying for, they will begin to look for someplace else to get it. Value creation in any organization is of supreme importance. Everything should lead to the creation of value. And yet, studies show that less than 50% of the energy consumed in most organizations contributes directly to the creation of value.

I remember years ago when everyone was trying to implement the concept associated with Total Quality Management (TQM), everyone became tasked with the job of identifying both our internal and our external customers. Since quality can only be defined by the customer, the only way we could know if we were producing quality was when our customer told us that we were. This introduced the "Voice of the Customer" to people in every corner of the organization. This was no doubt for me the most important outcome of the TQM years. The unintended negative consequence of this customer focus, however, was that often the external customer got lost in our quest to better serve our internal customers.

The voice of the principle *Create Value for Customers* advocates for the external customer. The only way to not lose this message in a cacophony of internal customer voices is to make certain there is clear, visual and constant alignment of what customers pay us to create. We will discuss this alignment in the next chapter under the principle called *Create Constancy of Purpose*.

Since quality can only be defined by customers, the only way we can know if we are producing quality is when our customers tell us that we are.

THE FOUNDATIONAL TRUTH ... *TRUST IS SACRED*

In a company where I worked at one time we went to great lengths to uncover very specific components of the value expected by our customers. We asked them what was most important and how they would determine if we were successful then we tried very hard to think about our work through the lens of each of these customer value components. When we finally got it right, our customers trusted that we would deliver exactly what we said we would, every single time and exactly when we said we would deliver it, no earlier and no later. (From the Just-in-time (JIT) years.)

I remember hearing once that a satisfied customer, one for whom we have earned their trust, tells three friends about it, but a customer who feels like his/her trust has been violated through our failure to get it right tells 3,000. If this is true, or even anything that approximates it, it speaks to the value of the trust an organization works so hard to create with its customers. A foundational truth then that sits below the principle of *Create Value for Customers* is that "Trust is Sacred." In other words, *because trust is sacred, therefore we Create Value for Customers.*

Once trust is lost, it may never be regained. This is why value creation through the lens of the customer must reign supreme in any enterprise. It is why it sits at the top of the pyramid and why anything that slows, interrupts, stops or even risks the loss of that trust must be seen as waste and all of the current and untapped potential of every employee must be directed toward maintaining trust. The voice of this principle is unmistakable and because we all know what it means to have people trust us, creating value for customers is very personal and when presented effectively always invokes the commitment of associates.

IDEAL BEHAVIORS … *FLOW VALUE TO CUSTOMERS*

Leaders

1. Ideally, every leader will be intimately familiar with what customers see as value added to them.
2. Conversations about customer values should be a regular part of leadership team meetings to make certain that every part of the organization is clear about what is the most important.
3. Leaders make certain that the organization structure, metrics, reward and recognition systems, communication systems, planning systems, training and development systems are perfectly aligned with the principles that lead to the continuous flow of value to external customers.
4. Every time leaders talk to managers and associates they are framing their conversations within the context of value to customers.
5. Leaders tell customers the truth and only make commitments they are capable of keeping.
6. Leaders ensure the acceleration of improvements within the organization to add greater and greater levels of value for customers.

Managers

1. In designing and building management systems, managers make certain that the voice of the customer is clearly recognized and integrated into key components of the systems.
2. Managers create opportunities for frontline associates to make a personal connection with customers and feel from their own experiences accountable to the customers for assuring the continuous flow of quality products and services.
3. Managers create metrics and visual systems that allow every associate to quickly be able to see whether they are winning or losing or getting worse or getting better relative to the value creation expectations of customers.

Frontline Associates

1. Every associate makes the effort to understand clearly the component of value they contribute and where they fit in the value stream.
2. Associates know how value should flow in their areas and are looking every day for barriers to the continuous flow of that value. Problems that are identified are immediately elevated to the appropriate levels.
3. Every associate takes personal responsibility for resolving barriers to the continuous flow of customer value. They do this by focusing on *what* is wrong rather than *who* is wrong and use the scientific method to make good decisions.
4. Associates collaborate with others, both peers and managers, in a way that creates the greatest likelihood of eliminating non-value added activities.

A NEW PARADIGM

Thirty years ago I saw an image of three overlapping circles showing Quality, Cost and Delivery. (See Figure 9.1.) The prevailing belief at that time was that a successful business had to choose one or perhaps two of these options for distinguishing themselves. The thinking was that if you were to be the low cost producer, you could not afford to do everything that was required to make things right the first time. Or if you wanted to be the best at delivery, the extra costs associated with special freight, less-than-truckload freight charges and just-in-case-inventory levels would keep you from being the lowest cost. Finally, if you wanted to be the best quality provider, the cost to accomplish this would surely make you uncompetitive in many markets.

The great news is that after 30 years or so, the most competitive companies are in fact those that can do all three. The secret to being able to do all three at once is the principle of *Flow Value to Customers*. It turns out that in order to become the highest quality supplier, you must eliminate every possible opportunity to create a defect. When you do that you are in a far better position to deliver exactly what the customer wants, and it also turns out that by speeding up and flowing the value creation process in response to actual demand, you must also have great first piece quality. Almost miraculously what it takes to create speed and quality also eliminates enormous amounts of waste and cost.

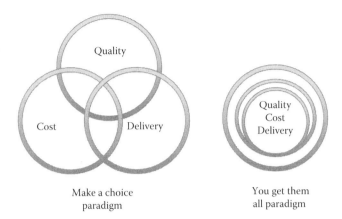

Make a choice
paradigm

You get them
all paradigm

FIGURE 9.1
Two opposing paradigms.

This transformation of paradigms does not happen overnight; it takes many years of continuous improvement effort but as soon as you begin the journey, you begin to reap the benefits. The further along the path you get, the more value that flows to the customer and to your shareholders.

SUMMARY

The voices of these two principles, *Create Value for Customers* and *Flow Value*, are powerful. Together they capture the most strategic view of organizational purpose. Understanding, communicating, organizing and flowing pure value to customers in a continuous, uninterrupted way captures in the four words *Flow Value to Customers* the essence of Enterprise Excellence. Listen carefully to these principles and they will guide you then support all of your efforts with the other eight principles found in the Shingo Model.

10

Embrace Scientific Thinking

The best decisions are based on facts and because humans are drawn to new things, they are curious about them and want to explore. Therefore we Embrace Scientific Thinking.

Earlier in this book we talked extensively about how the vulnerability that comes with humility enables learning in both an individual and an organization. Individuals who are humble are open to the possibility that they do not possess all knowledge, all skill or all power. *Humble* leaders acknowledge the probability that others, no matter their role, race or education are capable of solving problems of all kinds, simple or difficult, technical or human-related.

We have examined the inherent value of every individual in an organization, not just for his or her current capabilities, but also for their reservoir of untapped potential. *Respect* is not earned; it comes from being human. Trust and confidence on the other hand must be earned.

Knowing all of these things about the people who make up our workforce, the leader's role then is to create the conditions where people can pursue their natural instinct to want to always make things better, to continuously improve or in other words to *Seek Perfection*. We have discussed the natural sense of accountability people feel for doing things right, the first time, for *Assuring Quality at the Source* and eliminating all of the barriers that prevent them from continuously creating and *Flowing Value* in their work.

Because all of this is true, therefore leaders must also enable people's capacity to create value by providing a process for them to systematically and efficiently act on the knowledge and self-motivation that comes from hearing the voice of these principles. This chapter will describe a simple process for improvement called Scientific Thinking. Scientific Thinking becomes a principle by describing it in the form of an action. The principle is *Embrace Scientific Thinking.* The verb in the principle is embrace, meaning welcome it, reach out for it, encourage it and celebrate when someone demonstrates it. Scientific thinking is the predicate; it is what we embrace.

THE VOICE OF THE PRINCIPLE ...
EMBRACE SCIENTIFIC THINKING

While all of the principles discussed up until now have had a significant philosophical foundation, the principle related to scientific thinking is more grounded in the value of a rigorous and systematic approach to exploration of new ideas and problem solving. That being said, learning to sincerely embrace this time-tested methodology is not easy to do and even harder to sustain over the long term. Throughout my career, this has been one of the hardest things for me to consistently do. I think this may have been the reason we selected the word "embrace," because we knew that most of us would have to fundamentally change our thinking about the value of this disciplined approach to work before we would do it consistently.

Scientific thinking is essentially what we teach our sixth grade children in their first science classes. In its simplest form scientific thinking consists simply of five steps. These steps can be described in hundreds of different ways with many valuable add-ons. The essential steps are simply:

1. Formulate the question, be curious about something, wonder what could be causing a problem or how something might be better and perhaps even formulate a hypothesis.
2. Gather and carefully analyze all related facts, data and information.
3. Come to well-reasoned conclusions and test them against some criteria or standard (think principle).
4. Consider thoughtfully and objectively all other possibilities to affirm your conclusions.

5. Effectively share your conclusions with others.
6. Begin immediately to formulate your next questions and hypothesis for testing.

This is the scientific process that reveals reality and leads to smart conclusions and actions. Great scientists, having come to a conclusion, don't just take off the lab coat and go home, but they immediately begin to wonder what else, or what if or what would it take. The scientific process facilitates our natural inclination to want to make things better by providing a systematic way to continuously consider "what's next."

When the voice of this principle is deeply embedded into the culture, we will create an army of scientists in every organization who are insatiably curious about the possibilities and have the discipline and skills to think critically and act based on facts and data.

By Embracing Scientific Thinking, we create an army of scientists who are curious, disciplined and skilled to think critically and act based on facts and data.

The process of scientific thinking is often represented not linearly but as arrows in a continuous circle. As illustrated on the next page, the simplest version of this combination of scientific thinking and continuous improvement is represented by the PDCA cycle taught by Dr. Deming (Figure 10.1).

P – Plan. Plan includes most of the basic steps of scientific thinking, namely define a problem and if possible formulate a hypothesis, gather all relevant facts, data and information and critically analyze it. Based on findings develop a plan of action.
D – Do. Implement the plan including the development of goals and standards to which the actual results can be compared. Create a system for collecting data to determine if the action taken has had the anticipated impact.
C – Check. Follow up. Look at all relevant facts, data and information and decide to what degree the solution that was implemented solved the problem that you began with.
A – Act or Adjust. Based on what you have learned, formulate a new plan for how to improve the implemented solution so that results come closer to the target or the standard.

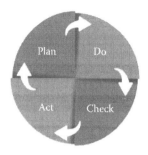

FIGURE 10.1
Basic PDCA cycle. (From Deming, W. E., *Out of the Crisis*. Cambridge, MA: Massachusetts Institute of Technology, Center for Advanced Engineering Study, 1986.)

THE FOUNDATIONAL TRUTHS ... *EMBRACE SCIENTIFIC THINKING*

There are least two foundational truths that become the why for this principle and make it universal and timeless. First, that the best decisions are made based on a clear understanding of reality; and second, that humans are drawn to new things, are curious about them and want to explore. Because both of these things are true we *Embrace Scientific Thinking*.

> *The best decisions are made based on a clear understanding of reality; humans are drawn to new things, are curious about them and want to explore.*

TRUTH ONE ... *THE BEST DECISIONS ARE ALWAYS MADE BASED ON A CLEAR UNDERSTANDING OF REALITY*

Often in business important decisions are made based on intuition, experience, bias or perhaps even prejudice. Millions of dollars are spent and sometimes businesses are even bought and sold based not on facts but inferences, assumptions or preferences.

Many well-known corporate leaders are very proud of their intuition or "gut." I believe there is some value to this kind of intuition, but it is best applied after a careful study of all of the facts. When more than one alternative action seems possible based on careful analysis of all the information at hand, only then might intuition, or your "gut," have a place.

At one point in my career I was Vice President for Manufacturing Engineering in a large company. The CEO announced one day that he had just bought a business and we were to transfer the production of our most cherished product to that facility to be made by the new employees. No research, no due diligence, no financial analysis, no capability studies and no scientific thinking. The factory was an old Civil War era three-story building nestled on the bend of a beautiful river. During the war it was used to make woolen blankets and the blue dye was still evident in the hard wood of all three floors. The only way to produce our products required moving them from floor to floor up and down an old elevator. At that point in my career I was still learning how to develop teams of "Master Problem Solvers," and this "gut decision" generated plenty of problems that certainly would have been avoided with just a little bit of scientific thinking.

TRUTH TWO ... HUMANS ARE CURIOUS AND WANT TO EXPLORE

The second foundational truth is that humans are drawn to new things, are curious about them and want to explore. Curiosity is at the front end of the process for scientific thinking and because I have five children and at last count 18 grandchildren, I know a bit about curiosity. I love how curiosity is described by Dr. Bruce Perry, associated with Alberta Mental Health. He said,

> Children are such curious creatures. They explore, question, and wonder, and by doing so, learn. From the moment of birth, likely even before, humans are drawn to new things. When we are curious about something new, we want to explore it. And while exploring we discover.*

I worked with a company once that generated and implemented nearly 200 improvement ideas per employee every single year. To enable this incredible rate of improvement, leaders and managers had created powerful management systems that supported the entire process of empowering teams to act quickly on each of their own ideas. By eliminating the

---

* Bruce Duncan Perry, MD, PhD. *Curiosity: The Fuel of Development*, Scholastic Inc.

barriers to making change, employees became very skilled at formulating a hypothesis, conducting simple experiments using the scientific process, and continuously exploring their almost limitless curiosity. Because they had proven their ability to make good decisions, management gave them a great deal of latitude to make almost every decision related to their jobs.

The reason why we "embrace" scientific thinking is because it enables the curiosity of people, and being able to act on that curiosity shows respect and helps people to reach more of their potential. When people convert potential to current capabilities, everybody wins.

Being able to act on curiosity shows respect and helps people to reach more of their potential.

A common problem for leaders trying to *Embrace Scientific Thinking* occurs when people focus on PDCA as a tool and the principle takes on a purely mechanical process. People often use the PDCA without thinking about why they are doing it. When this happens, following the rigor of the scientific process becomes a burden, slows things down, and eventually is resented and eventually abandoned.

The reason why the voice of this principle is so important is because the best decisions are made based on a clear understanding of reality and humans are drawn to new things, are curious about them, and want to explore. Because a rigorous exploration of new ideas using a disciplined approach leads to good ideas and good decisions, therefore we *Embrace Scientific Thinking.*

IDEAL BEHAVIORS ... *EMBRACE SCIENTIFIC THINKING*

Leaders

1. Leaders who *Embrace Scientific Thinking* believe deeply in the people who do the work in their organizations and challenge them to explore new ideas.
2. Leaders continuously focus on learning, both from success and failure. Failure is understood to be a natural part of exploration and experimentation and is acknowledged as such. People are encouraged to experiment within limits without fear of retribution for failure.

3. Leaders take an interest in people's experiments, go to the *Gemba*, ask questions and listen intently to what people are doing and learning.
4. Leaders create management systems that lead to important decisions only after rigorous analysis of facts and data and all relevant principles have been accounted for.

Managers

1. Managers ensure that every associate is educated in the value and tools associated with scientific thinking and have the team and group process skills to make a meaningful contribution to experimentation projects.
2. Managers organize work so that people have some time available to participate.
3. Managers coach teams in use of the PDCA cycle and ask questions that require teams to think outside of the box and propose solutions in line with the principles of Operational Excellence.
4. Managers watch for and recognize individuals and teams that take appropriate risks, and do the appropriate amount of analysis using facts and data.
5. Managers guide associates in selection of the most impactful experiments that will move the organization closer to continuously flowing value to customers.

Frontline Associates

1. Associates are curious, think, offer suggestions and learn how to think through the lens of the PDCA.
2. Associates demonstrate respect for peers and managers in their participation on teams involved in the improvement process.
3. Associates take risks by being willing to do things they have never done before, then learn from it and are willing to share what they learned with others.

SUMMARY

One might think that this principle is relatively easy to implement because it is somewhat mechanical rather than philosophical. It is more skill-based rather than belief-based and this argument has some merit. However, scientific thinking takes structure and discipline. It takes a willingness to take the time to reveal all of the relevant facts and avoid jumping to conclusions.

Perhaps the most compelling reason to embrace scientific thinking is its capacity to enable the curiosity and potential of people. Knowing how to evaluate the efficacy of an idea before recommending it builds trust, and using scientific thinking to ensure an effective implementation creates success. What organization wouldn't want great employees who have a continuous flow of well-vetted ideas and who know how to implement them in a way that has the greatest likelihood of success?

11

Principles of Enterprise Alignment

The one constant in a sea of change are the principles that inform our strategies and guide our decision-making.

Not all principles affect the roles of people in an organization the same. For example leaders have a far greater impact on the principles of *Respect for Every Individual* and *Lead with Humility* than do frontline associates. Certainly the principles apply to everyone, but the behavior of leaders relative to these principles profoundly impact the way others behave and ultimately the culture of the entire enterprise.

The operational principles related to continuous improvement like *Seek Perfection, Flow Value* and *Embrace Scientific Thinking* speak more loudly to managers and frontline associates than they do for senior leaders. All principles always apply to everyone, but during the course of everyday work, the principles in the center of the model, principles of continuous improvement, touch managers and associates more directly than they do top management.

Ensuring that the three principles at the top of the Shingo Pyramid find voice in the organization is again more directly on the shoulders of senior management. No one has the breadth of direct visibility to the entire enterprise or has influence on the stability of organizational direction quite like the team of senior executives. Senior management also plays a key role in ensuring the voice of the customer never gets lost in the bureaucracy of the organization.

This chapter will focus specifically on the remaining two principles identified in the Shingo Model (Figure 11.1): *Think Systemically* and *Create Constancy of Purpose*. They are found in the Shingo Model under the heading of Enterprise Alignment. *Create Value for the Customer* was previously discussed in conjunction with the principle of *Flow Value*.

FIGURE 11.1
Principles identified in the Shingo Model. (Copyright Utah State University.)

THE VOICE OF THE PRINCIPLE ... *THINK SYSTEMICALLY*

I often smile when people describe this principle as Think "System*atically*." While this is a good thought, "systematically" pertains more to scientific thinking and is very different than *Thinking Systemically*. I always try to kindly correct them; it is a mistake easily made before the voice of the principle becomes clearer. To think systemically is to always consider the connectedness of things. Everything is part of some system, affects that system and is affected by it. If you change one part of a system, chances are pretty good that you will affect the other parts. Not always directly and not always immediately, but sooner or later the reasons why individual items are part of the system, bring about some impact on the whole.

The voice of this principle speaks to leaders, managers and associates reminding us not to act on initiatives or solve problems in isolation. The root cause for a problem is often found not at the place the problem is experienced, but rather is likely to have originated somewhere else. Failure to solve problems at the systemic level may be faster and much easier but usually ends up only treating the symptoms.

Years ago, I remember struggling with this problem in a conference room as we were trying to solve a significant problem. I remember listening to the conversation and converting what I was hearing into the following picture illustrated in Figure 11.2.

Function   A   B   C   D   E

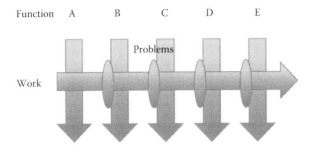

FIGURE 11.2
Problems at the boundaries.

What became clear from this conversation was that individually, the functions did a great job but almost every problem we were experiencing happened at the intersections between the work and the functions. When we looked at the key management systems that drove most of what we did, there was almost no structure to cause or even encourage us to work on problems together.

Organizational structure is a management system. We organize ourselves in a certain way for many reasons. Once this is done it is almost like we seal everything into place with a topcoat that keeps anything from moving, ever. The system for organization design is based on prevailing paradigms and once established, the structure becomes self-sustaining. The principle of *Thinking Systemically* is a paradigm breaker. When we *Think Systemically* we must confront many long-held traditions that have kept too many of us thinking functionally rather than the way work really flows.

> *When we Think Systemically we must confront many long-held traditions that have kept too many of us thinking functionally rather than the way work really flows.*

THE FOUNDATIONAL TRUTH ... *THINK SYSTEMICALLY*

The principle of *Thinking Systemically* is based on two very important foundational truths. First, that through understanding the relationships and interconnectedness within a system we make better decisions; and second, that as we see how and why everything is connected to, or part of something else, we can better predict and control outcomes. Because these statements are true, therefore we *Think Systemically.*

A leader has many ways to begin breaking down the barriers that prevent systemic thinking. A few of them are:

1. Make greater use of cross-functional teams to solve problems.
2. Make sure that cross-functional teams have the right people on them and the charter clarifies why they are on the team.
3. Routinely invite representatives from other groups to your team meetings to listen to your plans and offer an outside point of view.
4. Build into every management and work system some component that gets people who have different functional perspectives face to face.
5. When you hear of good work being done in a functional area outside of yours, take your team and meet with them to learn what they have done and why they do it.
6. When a key job opening occurs fill it with someone from outside of the functional area where the opening is. This takes patience, courage and respect for the untapped potential of people.
7. Create temporary "internships" that bring people from outside your area for a specific project or a short period of time to get an out of the box solution.
8. Form a company bowling/softball/soccer team and require participants to come from every functional group in the organization. Don't compete the sales team against the production team.

These are the easy options. In many (strike that) a few businesses I have seen, leaders have dealt with the need for systemic thinking head-on. Organizations have literally been turned on their side and reconstituted, shifting the accountability of the team from the functions to the way that value actually flows to the customer.

This is where the principle of *Thinking Systemically* intersects with the principle of *Flow Value*. One way to think about this is to start with the description of what is value and how does that value flow? As previously discussed lean thinkers often describe this as the "Value Stream." Value to customers almost always flows horizontally while functions are organized vertically. Many arguments for remaining functionally oriented can be made but most are based on old and out of date paradigms. The number of problems that can be solved with any one paradigm diminishes over time and only new paradigms can create breakthrough thinking and competitive differentiation.

The number of problems that can be solved with any one paradigm dimin-
ishes over time and only new paradigms can create breakthrough thinking
and competitive differentiation.

Breaking the old rules is not easy, particularly when it comes to organizational structure. This is a case where leaders need to speak the language
of the principle very clearly.

When I teach this principle in the classroom I often stand on a chair
and observe the group from a different perspective and invite others to
do the same thing. (Safety experts usually gasp!) The higher you get in an
organization the broader perspective you have. It is easier to see the connectedness of the individual components when you view it from higher in
the organization.

After college when I was working for John Deere I received my first super-
visory position. Our team of about six people was responsible for what was
called "stock sizing." We were building combines which had hundreds of
unique parts made out of sheet metal, so our job was to take the engineering drawings for each part and considering material thickness, bend radii,
etc. determine the appropriate size of sheet stock to start with. We were getting ready to produce a brand new combine and beginning with the right
stock size was critical. (We didn't have CAD systems back then.)

Most of the team members had been performing that function for
many years; I was the new kid on the block and naturally had many questions. Some team members clearly resented the fact that a very young and
very green "engineer" had become their supervisor. Some of my questions
included: what is the machine that will be used to form these parts; how
are these drawings you are making of the flat stock used and by who; how
is the tooling manufactured; how does this part fit into the combine, etc.?

To my surprise, almost no one could answer any of these basic questions.
They had been taught how to do the math and make the drawings necessary for toolmakers but that was about it. They had been doing it the same
way for many, many years. What was most shocking was that almost none
of them had ever been to the factory where the actual sheet metal blanks
were sheered from the coil stock, watched the bend brakes get set up or seen
them perform the actual bends. None had been to the final assembly line to
look at the fit and finish of the sheet metal parts they were affecting.

One afternoon I decided we would all spend the rest of the day at the
Gemba. We put away our slide rules (honest) and spent three hours visiting all
of the places that our work touched. I had made arrangements for engineers,

tool designers, production managers and production workers to meet us at various places to teach us what they did and to discuss possible implications of the stock sizing function on their work. From that time forward, the stock sizing team was never the same. People had lots of ideas for how they could improve their work, and their new supervisor became a *contributing* member of the group. Long after this event was completed people, continued to talk about what they saw and thanked me for making this happen.

IDEAL BEHAVIORS ... *THINK SYSTEMICALLY*

Leaders

1. Leaders are always challenging people to think of implications beyond their own functional boundaries.
2. Leaders look for every opportunity possible to give people the bigger picture and show people where and how they fit in.
3. Leaders challenge old paradigms, ask hard questions, listen to the input of others and explore organizational alternatives that better align work with value creation.
4. (See the list from earlier in the chapter.)

Managers

1. Managers create cross-functional teams to solve problems.
2. Managers design and build systems that require systemic thinking by everyone who uses them.
3. Managers avoid making decisions until they have systematically considered upstream and downstream implications on actions they may take.

Frontline Associates

1. Associates make the effort to understand areas outside of the one they happen to be working in.
2. Associates watch for actions that need to be changed but never seem to. They wonder what paradigms keep them from changing and ask their managers why.

THE VOICE OF THE PRINCIPLE ...
CREATE CONSTANCY OF PURPOSE

"The only thing that is certain is death and taxes" turns out to not be entirely correct; the statement should say "death, taxes and principles."

Of all the principles we discovered in creating the Shingo Model, *Create Constancy of Purpose* was the only one that was described as we found it exactly in the form of a principle. Edwards Deming, in his now famous 14 Points, described this principle as a statement of action that is grounded in foundational truths, is universal and timeless and governs outcomes. His full statement was to *"Create constancy of purpose* toward improvement of product and service, with the aim to become competitive, stay in business and to provide jobs (Deming 1985)."

Most of the writing I have seen on this, the first of his 14 Points, have to do with the outcomes, improvement, competitiveness or job creation, rather than the principle itself, which is *Create Constancy of Purpose.* The nugget in the statement is often lost.

Instability, or a constant change in purpose, is something that most of us are all too familiar with. At the enterprise level constancy of purpose is typically less of an issue than it is at the operating or sub-unit level. At this level constancy of purpose can take on a slightly narrower lens to include

- Constancy of direction
- Constancy of strategy
- Constancy of policy
- Constancy of systems
- Constancy of performance metrics
- Constancy of management personnel

Constancy does not mean that these things never change. On the contrary, as Henry Ford put it 70 years ago:

To decree that today's standard shall be tomorrow's is to exceed our power and authority. Such a decree cannot stand. We see all around us yesterday's standards, but no one mistakes them for today's. Today's best, which superseded yesterday's, will be superseded by tomorrow's best. (Ford and Crowther 1926).

Henry Ford was talking about standards but the wisdom well applies to purpose, direction, strategy, policy, systems, metrics and management. The tightrope between the principles of *Creating Constancy of Purpose* and *Seek Perfection* (continuous improvement) is a tricky one. This paradox I believe is what Henry Ford was talking about. People and organizations need a standard which they can aspire to and from which they can measure improvement. Having a standard does not mean that the standard does not change. As capabilities increase and goals are met, new standards should be developed that become the new targets.

Constancy of purpose means simply that a standard is indeed created; people know what it is and everything points to the standard, that is until it is raised. Constancy does not necessarily mean the same for long periods of time. It does mean that everyone knows what it is, how they impact it, how they are performing to it and when they are ready to raise the bar. Direction, vision and why we exist should not change very often; operating targets may.

THE FOUNDATIONAL TRUTHS ...
CREATE CONSTANCY OF PURPOSE

This principle is grounded on three foundational truths that sit below the principle and make it universal and timeless

1. Humans want to be a part of something and know that they are making a difference.
2. Success depends on a commitment to a shared understanding of why we exist.
3. An unwavering clarity of organizational purpose, direction and strategy enables people to innovate, adapt and take risks with greater confidence.

Because these things are true, therefore we *Create Constancy of Purpose*.

Organizational purpose should be clearly communicated to every single person affected by and who can affect the outcomes. It is hard to conceive of anyone on the payroll of an organization that would not benefit from knowing where the organization they work for is going and what is important to get it there. People want to make a difference and every one of them is laden with not only current capabilities but also untapped potential.

I know of a company that manufactures air bags for the automotive industry. They describe their purpose as "Saving Lives" and ask every one of their employees every day, "What have I done today to save more lives?" Everything they do is connected with this shared statement of purpose. Another company says their purpose is to "Make Life Better." This is a company that manufactures a basic commodity for the gas, oil and mining industry. To them, while they are dedicated to their customers and value creation, they have built a powerful culture based on the purpose of making life better: better for customers, better for shareholders, better for employees and their families and better for the communities where they work.

Being certain in the knowledge of direction and strategy unlocks the potential of people, freeing them to innovate with confidence and take the lead in creating the next higher standard of excellence.

Being certain in the knowledge of direction and strategy unlocks the potential of people, freeing them to innovate with confidence and take the lead in creating the next higher standard of excellence.

I have never seen *Constancy of Purpose* more clearly illustrated than in an organization I recently visited with a client. I had actually visited them two years prior. As soon as anyone entered the facility, they immediately became aware of why the company existed and the strategy to get there.

Clearly, as good as they were when I first saw them, as we walked the facility with the top management team now two years later, there was evidence everywhere of how their purpose was being deployed into every work area. Metrics were aligned to this purpose from top to bottom and across all elements of the business. Everything was visible to everyone. Every person we talked to could describe exactly how they contributed to the company goals and could show at their places of work whether they were getting better or worse at their unique value contribution to the purpose. We heard many teams describe the projects they were working on and in each case they could explain exactly how their latest improvement ideas made a difference. Pictures on the walls showed smiling people being recognized for great ideas for improvement.

When diverse people share a common vision and are aligned on how to get there, their diversity becomes a powerful source for innovation. The clarity and confidence that comes from listening to the voice of the principle of *Creating Constancy of Purpose* in any organization, like standardization in the words of Henry Ford, creates a culture where people are sure of themselves, become better collaborators on projects and make investments better suited for the long term.

When diverse people share a common vision and are aligned on how to get there, their diversity becomes a powerful source of innovation.

PRINCIPLES THEMSELVES
CREATE CONSTANCY OF PURPOSE

Few things can *Create Constancy of Purpose* like principles. Because principles are universal and timeless they are in fact the ultimate expression of *Constancy of Purpose*. Large multinational corporations span many different cultures and employ people from literally every kind of background and personal value set. No matter what we wish, business in Siberia is not the same as in Samoa. Customers are not the same in Vietnam as they are in New York City and employees are different in Arkansas than they are in San Francisco. With all of these differences we can take great comfort in the fact that the exact same principles that speak to value creation in one situation apply equally to any other. How we apply them will be different for sure, but the miracle of principles is that they are indeed universal and timeless.

As customers change, markets change, managers change, strategy changes and employees change, the one thing that we know will be constant in this sea of change are the principles that speak to all of us every day and influence the formation of our strategies and guide our decision-making. The old adage, "The only thing that is certain is death and taxes," turns out to not be entirely correct; the statement should say "death, taxes *and principles.*"

How we apply them will be different for sure, but the miracle of principles is that they are indeed universal and timeless.

At the company I was just describing, when we met in a conference room to talk towards the end of the day, several key managers made a somewhat formal presentation on a host of topics. At the bottom of each PowerPoint slide was a small symbol illustrating the principle that this topic related to the most and had been informed by. For every person, every day, everywhere, the principles of Operational Excellence were *Creating Constancy of Purpose* and consistently guiding every aspect of their very successful business.

IDEAL BEHAVIORS ... *CREATE CONSTANCY OF PURPOSE*

Leaders

1. Leaders set direction then continuously communicate that direction in many different ways and on every opportunity possible.
2. Leaders, when receiving proposals for projects, ask how this initiative supports the organizational purpose and moves it closer to its vision. The leader spearheads these conversations and requires these connections be clear and visible.
3. Leaders create a scorecard that balances all aspects of the business, both results and behaviors, and makes certain that the scorecard is deployed from top-to-bottom and side-to-side.

Managers

1. Managers talk to employees every day about the purpose of the organization and help employees to see how they fit in.
2. Managers create scoreboards that are linked and aligned with higher-level goals and help associates to see how their work links upward.
3. Managers create visual management systems that are simple, visual and end-to-end.

Frontline Associates

1. Associates use the scoreboards to keep track of their progress.
2. Associates participate in discussions about their numbers and share ideas with others.
3. Associates make an effort to understand the mission, vision and guiding principles of the organization and apply them to their work.

SUMMARY

As is obvious from the significance of the ideal behaviors related to these two principles, leaders play an essential role in *Thinking Systemically* and

Creating Constancy of Purpose. I was asked by the CEO of a privately held global consumer products company to help him prepare his relatively young children to assume significant positions of responsibility in the company. Over almost three years it was extremely gratifying to see them gravitate to the principles. They had been taught great values from a very young age so hearing principles for them was a natural progression of their personal and leadership development.

Near the end of my work with them their father was beginning to let go of many operational details and began to think more philosophically about the family company. In an off-site meeting where we were working on defining the company purpose, the next generation of leaders concluded that they had done an excellent job but felt that the next step was to take their ideas to the employees and get their input on what the company's purpose and vision should be.

I was proud of their intentions, but suggested that purpose is probably not something to be put to the masses to reach consensus on, especially in a private company. Establishing the reason for being, knowing how to talk about it clearly, passionately and relentlessly is a leadership role that cannot be delegated or abdicated to anyone else. Naturally when others know what it is and have had an opportunity to align their own thinking to it, they too will become advocates for *Creating Constancy of* the organizational *Purpose.*

12

Leaders Lead Culture

What leaders really lead is culture.

Dave Petersen, CEO
The OC Tanner Company, 2012

Delegation by senior management for improvement of the business is an all too often and very unfortunate unintended and almost always negative consequence of distilling principles down to tools and systems. When business improvement is seen as training people on the use of some new tools, diffusing a few improvement systems or organizing some project teams to fix things, it is easy for senior leaders to opt themselves out.

While tools, management systems and good people are necessary requirements for creating business improvement, they are hardly sufficient for creating a sustainable culture of excellence. Many studies have shown over and over again that the vast majority (70%) of business improvement programs have not been sustained over the long term. Inevitably, well-intentioned initiatives get sidetracked or derailed during the normal course of events in any enterprise.

Here is a list of some of the reasons I have experienced for why programs lose their way. You can no doubt add to this list from your own experiences.

1. Leaders get promoted, terminated or just move on, and replacements often have their own ideas about how things should be done.
2. Leadership teams read a new book or listen to a new consultant with new and better ideas for how to make business improvements.
3. Economies get bad and staff-type manpower that is usually doing the work of improvement gets laid off.

4. Economies get better and the urgency that once created the improvement initiatives is suddenly lost in the face of increasing revenues and better opportunities somewhere else.
5. Normal business opportunities and problems that are urgent overtake improvements that are important and more long-term.
6. Associates working in the improvement areas get great exposure both within and outside of the company and are recruited away.
7. Associates working in the improvement areas become frustrated that they do not get the management support they believe is necessary to make the changes they want to make and leave, or worse, quit and stay.

When business improvement, a crucial element of any enterprise, is seen as something else to be done on the list, the probability of it being sustainable over the long term is very low. Business improvement must become a part of every person's work responsibilities. Stated another way, continuous business improvement must become a normal part of a culture of enterprise excellence. If improvement is allowed to become just another item on a list of tasks for someone to do, it will invariably not get done.

LEADERS LEAD CULTURE

I heard David Petersen, the CEO of the OC Tanner Company in Salt Lake City say that, "What leaders really lead is culture." To lead culture, leaders must become competent at observing, evaluating and influencing the behavior of others. For leaders to lead culture, they must recognize the special trust given to them that obligates them to their followers. While above others on a traditional organization chart, they are equals in most respects and servants in many others.

For leaders to lead culture, they must recognize the special trust given to them that obligates them to their followers.

Leaders are the only people in the organization who can effectively teach managers and other associates correct principles. They teach principles in a hundred ways with essentially everything they do: every employee interaction, every problem to be solved, every strategic initiative to be embarked on, every management system used. Even a routine report to associates or board leaders presents an opportunity for a leader to teach guiding principles. Leaders teach principles literally through conversations but equally and perhaps even more importantly, leaders teach principles by role modeling the ideal behaviors associated with the principles. The voice of each and every principle must flow through the voice of the leader, every day.

The voice of each and every principle must flow through the voice of the leader, every day.

For many years I have been closely associated with a great company in the automotive industry. This company is a strategic supplier to Toyota. Toyota has a policy that top managers must retire when they turn 60 years of age unless specifically invited by the President to stay on for a special assignment. Often these assignments include being assigned to one of their strategic suppliers to teach them the principles, systems and tools used inside of Toyota.

My friends in this supplier company report that their assigned Toyota teacher lived, worked and taught them every day for nearly five years. What was most interesting is that they say he never once told them what to do. He taught almost exclusively with questions. He would say things like, "What do you see happening here? Why do you think that is happening? What do you think is the root cause? How can you be sure? Do you have data to support your conclusion? What else might you do? Have you seen the problem with your own eyes? Show me! What are the alternatives to resolve this problem? Are you sure? What else? What is the principle that governs the outcome we are seeing? Who are the right people to be involved in this solution? When do you think you will be able to answer that question? What will it take to be certain that it never happens again?" and on and on.

Always requiring people to think for themselves, never taking the monkey off of the leaders', managers' or associate's backs for owning both the problem and the solution, the Toyota surrogate never stopped demonstrating and teaching principles of humility, respect, continuous improvement, enterprise alignment and customer value by what and how he taught.

The point here is that leaders do not need to feel the burden of being the experts in all things, far better that they become the experts in asking the best questions. Since leaders lead culture, leaders should be able to ask questions that teach and reinforce the voice of principles that form the foundation of the culture and help to *Create Constancy of Purpose*.

I know of the leader in a company who established a policy requiring every capital appropriation request be supported with a discussion of the key principles affecting the problem they are trying to solve with money. Managers had to be able to describe the problem or opportunity in the context of principles either being followed or ignored and explain why the money was needed to solve the problem. Further, requesting managers had to show how the money would be used in harmony with guiding principles. Failing to do this resulted in the capital request being denied.

The best leaders I have known never take their eyes off of the results scorecard, but also provide a way to be constantly reminded to look for and reinforce ideal behaviors.

REQUIREMENTS OF LEADERS WHO LEAD CULTURE

The senior leaders in any enterprise have the most profound impact on its culture. For the culture to become something other than what it is, leaders must do at least the following three things:

1. *See Reality*
2. *Be Principled*
3. *Balance the Scorecard*

LEADERS SEE REALITY

The first and very often most difficult step in leading culture is to learn to see the behaviors that represent the culture. It is surprising how hard this is to do when we are programmed to observe and think in the context of work and results. It has taken me almost ten years to shift my lens so that I see behaviors, not process or results, and occasionally I still get hooked. Behaviors are actions that are observable, recordable and measurable, and leaders must learn to see them through the paradigms related to culture.

An important part of teaching leaders and managers to see behavior and measure culture is asking them to go to the *Gemba* and look for behavioral evidence of a specific concept they are trying to understand, such as *Assuring Quality at the Source*. As clearly as I know how, I remind them that they are not going to the *Gemba* to observe the work; they are going to look for a specific set of behaviors in the context of the work.

The first time they go out, no matter how many times I remind them, they always come back literally gushing with information about the *work* that people do, how they do it (how the process works), the specific roles of each person, how well they are doing at delivering the outcomes they are accountable for and eventually a little bit about a few behaviors.

Returning to the classroom, participants convene in table groups to share and analyze what they have seen. With my coaching, invariably they conclude that they didn't ask very good questions about behavior. What they discover is that they quickly gravitated to some observable artifact related to the work and then immediately became hooked in the content of the work. Most leaders and managers find it easy to ask lots of questions about work content and process but very difficult to think about and see behavior. I know it seems odd but try it.

One very senior executive said to the group after their third unsuccessful attempt at observing behaviors, "We suck at this!" Don't laugh too loudly until after you have tried to do the same thing. Learning to see behavior when we have spent entire careers focusing on results is not as easy as it sounds like it should be.

Observing leaders and managers struggle to have great conversations that reveal behaviors, even in a controlled setting, constantly reminds me just how hard it is to notice behaviors in the day to day heat of doing the work. This sounds almost impossible to believe, such a simple thing as observing something that is as obvious as a behavior. Time after time, in almost every industry and on almost every continent, I have seen the same thing: leaders and managers having difficulty switching from observing the work, the process and the results to also observing the way the people are behaving in their effort to produce these results.

Often in the classroom people will say things like, "I imagine this would be really tough in XXX country. They really have a top-down culture where considering people and behaviors would be the last thing on their minds." The reality is that I have done this exercise with leaders in Mexico, Brazil, Venezuela, China, Japan, England, Scotland, Ireland, Canada, Denmark and Sweden, to mention only a few, and have observed no noticeable difference in their deeply ingrained tendency to primarily see process and results.

The good news is that like everything, something that is difficult the first time can with practice become second nature over time. Key to observing behavior is learning what to ask. The question I often ask myself first that helps get on the right track is, "This result is not what I would have expected. I wonder what behavior is contributing to this outcome?" This question opens the door to probe into the actual behaviors, some of which may be immediately visible and some of which may be hidden.

Watch for how people respond to their leader when questioned about something. Ask people to explain why they do what they do. Observe them in meetings: who talks, who do people look at, how well do they listen to each other, how are decisions made? Do people come prepared to contribute? Do people look into your eyes when they talk to you? Are they eager to share or is having a conversation an agonizing experience for both of you? How do people use email? What happens when something goes wrong? What do people do to engage others? What do people do when they have an idea?

There is no end to the questions and observations that can be made that reveal behaviors. Usually one question begets another and then another until a clear pattern of behaviors begins to reveal itself. Once the actual behaviors start to become clear, a second question is often helpful: "I wonder what is causing this behavior?"

> *Usually one question begets another and then another until a clear pattern of behaviors begins to reveal itself.*

Remember my story about the Japanese supervisors who had a secret communications system to quickly pass the word that the boss was coming. This elaborately contrived system gave them enough time to either get busy or to hide so they would not have to talk to the boss. I wonder what the leaders did to invoke such an extreme behavior in their associates.

People always act the way they do for a reason. As previously discussed, people act based on their beliefs and what they have come to value. If you observe that people tend to hide their mistakes, you must ask yourself, "Why would they not immediately notify their supervisor or manager when they discovered that a critical mistake had been made?" Consider the possibilities.

1. Perhaps a person has been severely disciplined in the past for making a mistake.
2. Perhaps they may have had their job threatened.
3. Perhaps they are protecting someone else.
4. Perhaps they are incented to produce volume and stopping because of a mistake would affect their personal income.
5. Perhaps they are members of a team and they do not want to let their team down.
6. Perhaps they are embarrassed or humiliated.

Each revelation invokes a unique and deeper set of successive questions until the root cause or causes for a behavior are revealed. Why has this person, or this group of people, come to value passing forward a known defect more than stopping and making the defect immediately visible? As your questions progress, the real root cause for people's choice of behavior will begin to become evident.

At this point, be careful not to just implement a technical solution to a fundamentally human and behavioral problem. This is taking the easy way out and without fundamentally changing the way people think about revealing problems or mistakes, people will always find a way to continue to act the way they always have.

Be careful not to just implement a technical solution to a fundamentally human and behavioral problem.

Max DePree, CEO at Herman Miller, often said, "The first responsibility of a leader is to see reality." For many years I did not understand what he meant by this but in recent years his wisdom and humility as a leader have become much clearer. People will not follow a leader whose perception of the way things are is jaded by their ego or their unwillingness to ask the hard questions or listen to what people say in response to them. To have followers, leaders must be able to see the world for what it is.

To have followers, leaders must be able to see the world for what it is.

Learning to see reality is not easy and is perhaps one of the main reasons that culture change is the most difficult work you will ever do. It is deeply personal for you as a leader and for every person you are asking to behave differently.

Seeing reality and knowing how to act in complex situations is both a gift and a skill. Wise behavioral choices are learned, usually over a long period of time. They are learned by

1. Being very centered in what you believe to be true and from that, what you value the most
2. Listening to wise council given at moments of vulnerability or openness
3. Deep reflection on the outcomes of past choices (both good and bad)
4. Watching the examples of others
5. Routinely following the regimen of a well-designed system that is aligned with principles

BE PRINCIPLED

I have often asked leaders, managers and associates to describe the attributes of the greatest leader they have ever worked with. While their answers were diverse, two common themes have emerged consistently over the years and in nearly every part of the world. First, great leaders lead with humility, and second, great leaders are guided in their actions by a clear set of principles.

> *Great leaders lead with humility and are guided in their actions by a clear set of principles.*

A principled leader demonstrates principle-based behavior to others. By being transparent and constantly explaining the principle that is governing his or her actions about why he or she does what they do, they are giving people the ability to think through their own options at a much higher level and make good decisions that are in the best interests of customers and the business. Principled people become capable of acting independently, with purpose and confidence. When leaders and the people they are responsible for understand and live by the principles that govern their outcomes, they become powerful, or said another way, they become empowered.

PRINCIPLE-BASED PLANNING

At one point in my evolution of thinking about the power of principles I likened the principled leader to a savant and used an image of someone with their hands over a crystal ball and seeing into the future. As a leader, wouldn't it be great if today we could see the long-term outcomes of our actions? Unfortunately, uncertainty is a natural part of all of our jobs. A significant part of why we create strategic and tactical plans is to identify the outcomes we want, then plan countermeasures for the risk we expect to experience.

> *When leaders and the people they are responsible for understand and live by the principles that govern their outcomes, they become powerful, or said another way, they become empowered.*

Armed with the clear voice of principles, in the strategic plan of a principled leader are considerations for all of the principles that affect the outcomes identified in the plan. The effect of each principle, when carefully considered, can create a much broader set of strategies taking into account both the technical and the behavioral requirements for success. Building great management systems based on those principles can help to drive the ideal behaviors required to achieve the desired results. I call this Principle-Based Planning.

When not using Principle-Based Planning, leaders remain naïve to the source of their anxieties and experience constant tension about the many things that could go wrong. Working under constant stress is not healthy for either the leader or the organization. I remember going to work right out of college and being shocked to see the long hours and weekends that so many of the managers worked. They constantly worried that whenever any of their employees were working, they would need to be there to solve their problems and make key decisions for them. Most of them smoked heavily, had problems with relationships and worked so many hours that they had no social life. If this is what happened when you moved up, I was pretty sure I wanted no part of it!

A principled leader who builds a principled team is also creating a culture where risk and stress are significantly reduced.

Leaders who become principled develop a very strong internal compass that points toward ideal behaviors. They become keenly aware of the standard they expect to see in themselves and others and the gap between ideal and reality becomes crystal clear, often even to the point that they forget to see how good they have become.

I am reminded of a great company I worked for at one point that had just such a behavioral standard. It seemed like the company was in constant turmoil as people's behavioral expectations of each other were so high. Senior management even seemed to be constantly held under a microscope by the people on the frontline. Astonishingly, the SMT, or senior management team, was just fine with that.

When visitors came to visit our company they would rave about how good we were and employees would inevitably shake their heads and say to each other, "Why do they say that? Can't they see how bad we are at this thing or that thing?" Over time our vision guided by our commitment to a few key principles had become so elevated and grown so clear that it was almost impossible to be satisfied with the status quo, no matter how good it was.

When we changed the criteria for receiving the Shingo Prize to become principle based, we had to raise the standard for receiving it three times in three years. It was difficult and a bit unfair to announce to companies in the middle of making an application that the criteria had changed. Once we knew better what excellence really looked like there was no way we could leave things as they were. This happened to us three times as our ability to hear the voice of the principles became sharper and sharper.

I worked with an organization once where I was teaching principles to the senior leadership team. When we went to the *Gemba* to observe their existing culture all five of the teams came back and ranked what they saw consistently between four and five on a scale where five was ideal. The third time they did this I knew I had to force them to raise their expectations, so I told them that the highest they could rate any behavior was a three and that they then had to describe what a principle-based five would look like beyond what they had seen. As they proposed behaviors they thought to be ideal I kept asking, "Yes, and what would make that even better, what would make it even more ideal?" Little by little their expectations began to elevate until they felt compelled to take actions never before even imagined that would create a far more excellent and sustainable culture. This took about two years to achieve!

The higher the standard that people aspire to, the more dissatisfied they become with performance that is anything less than the ideal. When my oldest daughter was about five years old we watched her pick out a simple tune on an old upright piano and naturally we thought she was destined to become a prodigy. Even though we couldn't afford it at the time, we picked out a beautiful new Yamaha six-foot grand piano for her to learn on.

Seventeen years later she was getting ready to perform her senior recital at university where she had majored in piano performance. I thought that everything she played was perfect no matter what piano she played on, but after graduation to my great disappointment she refused to play on any piano other than her Yamaha or a Steinway and would rarely just play for our friends and family unless she had the piece prepared perfectly. Her standard had become so high that all she could hear were the mistakes and the tone of the piano and all I could hear was the music.

The higher the standard that people aspire to, the more dissatisfied they become with performance that is anything less than the ideal.

So also it is with leaders who develop a deep understanding and commitment to guiding principles. They come to expect a Steinway performance and nothing less is satisfying. The good news is that any leader with hard work and discipline can create a senior recital capable performance from every one of their teams.

BALANCE THE SCORECARD

An organization that does not measure both sides of the equation is not balanced and does not have a balanced scorecard.

In the late '80s I remember going to a conference, hearing a speaker and buying his book on the balanced scorecard. Conventional thinking at that time and even today was that balance meant more than just financial metrics. Dutifully, most of us considered carefully all of the other things besides end of month, quarter or year measures of cost and profit.

To the financial metrics we eventually learned to add measurements of quality, service and people-related outcomes. Eventually we felt we had a pretty balanced scorecard, measuring the results of all of the major dimensions of the business.

Even though a balanced scorecard will likely be different in every organization, almost all have some version of these metrics: Quality, Cost, Service and Morale. Some businesses might also include safety, security or any other unique aspect of their business outcomes. What is universal is that the selected metrics for each of these categories are measurements of results. Business schools call these key *performance* indicators, or KPIs.

Even though most of us have had lots of experience measuring KPIs, I will list a few from each category. Look for the performance or result in each metric.

Quality Metrics

1. The number of defects per hundred, thousand or even millions of opportunities
2. The number of units returned by customers
3. The number of customer complaints over a specific period of time
4. The number of units that pass through the entire system right the first time without a single defect or correction

Cost Metrics

1. Cost per unit
2. Changes in cost over time
3. Material, labor and overhead costs
4. Sales dollars per employee
5. Inventory turns (raw, WIP or finished goods)
6. Turns on capital employed

Service Metrics

1. Lead time or cycle time from order to shipment
2. Length of time required to resolve customer calls
3. Number of customer calls resolved on the first call
4. Percentage of orders filled complete exactly to the promised date
5. Length of time waiting before seeing a doctor

Morale Metrics

Even metrics measuring employee morale are often created in the context of KPIs, or performance outcomes. Examples might include

1. The percentage of employees who say, "This is a great place to work"
2. The annual turnover of employees
3. The number of hours per employee per year spent in training
4. Number of promotions per year from internal sources
5. The number of improvement ideas implemented per employee

The purpose of these lists is not to suggest that these are not good or in some cases even great metrics, but rather to illustrate how they are all measurements of results. They are key indicators of performance or KPIs. They are measures of outcomes or indicators of what happened when we did something. If we did something well we got a great outcome, but if we didn't the outcome was not so great. By definition they are lagging indicators, calculation of the actual metric occurred after, sometimes long after the actual thing that caused it.

Proactive Metrics

In the cause and effect formula, KPIs are all effects; actions taken based on a study of the effects are reactive. But what about the causes, should they not also be measured? Being proactive suggests we should also measure behaviors since we have already established that behaviors have a profound impact on results. Ideal behaviors are informed by principles.

As we are learning to measure behavior we are also learning to measure culture even though many people say that culture is impossible to measure. Because what gets measured gets improved, every organization should have a metric or series of metrics that measure culture or behavior. A leader cannot build a sustainable culture of excellence unless they know if they are getting better of getting worse. Is their culture moving forward or is it moving backward?

A balanced scorecard including measurements of behavior helps the principled leader to be proactive in creating a high performance culture that is capable of sustaining ideal results over the long term.

A STANDARD FOR BEHAVIOR

To measure anything you must have a standard. For example, to measure distance you use a tape measure that contains a scale that is calibrated to a standard. Similarly to measure a weight you use a scale that is also carefully calibrated to a standard. The same with speed, sound, heat, cost, etc. The idea is that for a measurement to have validity and be useful, it must be based on a standard.

A standard is something that is recognized universally as the authoritative statement and acknowledged as the final say. When I was in graduate school I participated on a project with the National Institute for Standards and Technology (NIST). We were developing standards for Computer-Aided Manufacturing (CAM) systems. NIST has 2,500 employees and at least that many partner contractors, all dedicated to the creation of and promotion of standards...technical standards used to measure almost everything … but culture.

Measuring culture in a way that is recognized and valid requires a standard. The device used to measure culture is not a caliper, a micrometer or even something as sophisticated as a Computer-based Coordinate Measurement Machine (CMM). The standard used to measure culture cannot come from the beliefs of a single person or cannot be based on something that is not universally understood to mean the same thing.

Measurements of culture cannot be grounded in something that changes over time. Measurements of culture, which infer measurements of behavior, require a universally accepted behavioral scale that rises above all of these values related characteristics and must be universal, timeless and inarguable; enter principles. Principles provide the perfect framework for creating a scale from which culture can be consistently and reliably measured.

We spent several years at the Shingo Institute trying to develop a reliable scale based on principles from which companies could be evaluated. In the end we used our best understanding of an ideal behavior as the far right or best-case scenario. When we performed an organizational assessment we compared the behaviors that we were able to observe to the standard and created a score based on the degree to which the ideal, or standard, was evident throughout the entirety of the enterprise. Once examiners doing the assessments have the ability to clearly hear the voice of a principle, they never seem to have trouble evaluating the degree to which something measures up.

KEY BEHAVIORAL INDICATORS

The following are examples of what behavioral expectations might be on the balanced scorecard. You might want to call these KBIs or Key Behavioral Indicators.

Quality KBIs

To ensure quality, ideally you would expect

1. Every *leader* to demonstrate a continuous commitment to quality by placing it at the top of every priority list.
2. Every *leader* always ensures that actions taken in any situation never send a message that it might be okay to compromise quality.
3. *Managers* would make certain that quality systems are in place in every part of the organization, the systems are simple and visual, are being followed and that they are continuously improving.
4. *Associates* are rigorous about following known best practice in their work.
5. *Associates* always use designated tools for the job.
6. *Associates* immediately take corrective action when they see a condition that has the potential to result in an error or a defect.

Cost KBIs

To better manage and improve costs you would ideally expect that

1. Every *leader* provides managers and associates access to the information they need to fully understand the costs that they impact.
2. *Managers* provide the systems so that every associate can identify the waste within their scope of work. Managers then support the changes in management and work systems required to eliminate it.
3. *All* frontline *associates* use facts and data every day to visualize how they impact costs and take ownership for making improvements.

Delivery KBIs

To improve delivery results, it would be ideal if

1. *Leaders* were in constant and personal contact with customers to clearly understand and are able to articulate customer expectations in the context of the organization.
2. *Managers* assist associates in developing metrics that are specific to customer demand, simple and visual, achievable but also stretch thinking and continuously elevate improvements in results.
3. Frontline *associates* perform all of their work and make all decisions based on what is ultimately in the best interest of the customers.
4. All improvements made by frontline *employees* focus on everything, no matter how small, that might become a barrier to the flow of value to customers.

Morale KBIs

To improve employee morale, it would be ideal if

1. Every *leader* would always act as though they are a servant of the people and the customer.
2. A *leader's* natural ego can be set aside in favor of empowering every associate to grow and reach his or her full potential.
3. *Managers* would ideally spend most of their time in the *Gemba*, asking great questions, coaching for improvement and recognizing the accomplishments of others.
4. Every frontline *associate* takes personal responsibility for their work and becomes involved daily in efforts to improve.
5. Frontline *associates* offer their support to colleagues in an effort to lift the team's overall success.

These are examples of what might be seen as ideal behaviors or KBIs. I am certain that if each of you asked the question, "I wonder what would make these behaviors even better?" you would be able to expand and create even better examples of ideal behaviors for leaders, managers and associates. Be careful not to be too prescriptive in defining ideal behaviors. At the leadership level ideal behavioral statements should be broad and strategic, providing a framework that others can use to drill down into specific behaviors that become the targets for their specific work.

The exception to the above generalizations relate to their own work. Leaders should be very specific in establishing their own behavioral standards based on principles. Making both their standards and their assessments public will not only improve results, but also set a very high benchmark for others in the organization.

SUMMARY

Because creating results is the urgent part of any organization, it is a natural instinct for almost all leaders to focus their own energies and the capabilities of the organizations they lead on them. But culture and behaviors are the important! Culture is the critical enabler to almost every desired outcome, and great leaders learn to balance their focus on behaviors, the important, and results, the urgent. Proactive leaders make it their highest priority to focus on the ideal behaviors that lead to ideal results.

To be an effective leader of culture, a leader must be willing and able to tell the truth, or see reality. To see reality, a leader must be willing to go where work happens, be curious, ask sincere and challenging questions, and be humble enough to see the influence of their own behaviors in the behaviors of others.

Great leaders listen for and hear the voice of all relevant principles that affect the outcomes they are responsible for and make them a deep and lasting part of their personal compass. By listening to and being guided by the clear voice of principles, leaders raise personal and organizational standards of excellence to the ideal defined by the principle.

Great leaders balance the scorecard with metrics that focus the organization on both ideal results (KPIs) and the ideal behaviors (KBIs).

Leaders value the cultures they are responsible for and pay attention to the creation of an ideal and sustainable culture of enterprise excellence based on principles. There is no doubt that "What leaders really lead, is culture!"

13

Hearing the Voice of Principles

People may not perish from the lack of principles, but they certainly might perish under the weight of the bureaucracy required to govern the unprincipled.

SUMMARY OF KEY CONCEPTS

Before concluding let's review a few key concepts. Readers may feel I am being redundant since I have chosen to restate many of these important concepts several times throughout the book. Because I know that changing mindsets, beliefs and habits is not a one-seminar process, my approach to working with clients has been to teach a concept, see it in the real world, work on it for a few months, hear it again and then add something new. This process of repetition, application and soak time is laborious and requires a deep commitment but is the only way I know to really confront the personal transformation required of leaders to create a sustainable culture of excellence. For leaders, personal transformation must always precede organizational transformation.

Here is a brief summary of key concepts.

1. The only way to make significant business improvement sustainable is to change the culture.
2. To understand how to change the culture of an organization, you must understand how to help people change their behavior.
3. Our behaviors are a physical manifestation of our values or the things we value the most.
4. Our values inform our beliefs. Values and beliefs govern our behaviors.

5. Organizations are made up of people, all of whom have different values and hence different behaviors.
6. Principles are statements of action based on natural laws that govern outcomes.
7. Principles are universal and timeless because they are grounded in foundational truth.
8. The foundational truths behind principles usually reveal important attributes about the nature of human beings that principles are grounded in.
9. When people live by principles, they shift their focus from themselves to others.
10. The outcomes of people's behaviors based on their values are governed by principles.
11. Ideal behaviors are those that are most closely aligned with correct principles that lead to ideal results.
12. The most important responsibility a leader has is to help people learn to hear the voice of principles and make choices based on the principles that govern the outcomes they are responsible for.
13. Tools and systems are the ways we organize and execute work to create outcomes.
14. Aligning tools and systems with principles is often overlooked but is the most certain way of deploying principles into the day-to-day behaviors of people.
15. Principles rarely stand alone; usually multiple principles work together to effect outcomes.
16. Leaders have the greatest influence on the principles of *Respect for Every Individual, Lead with Humility, Think Systemically, Create Constancy of Purpose* and *Create Value for Customers.*
17. Manager and frontline associates have the greatest impact of the principles of *Seek Perfection, Assure Quality at the Source, Flow Value, Focus on Process* and *Embrace Scientific Thinking.* Leaders also have great influence on the principle of *Seek Perfection.*
18. Every principle has a voice that speaks to those who will listen to it. Learning to listen and act in harmony with principles is a lifelong process. Individuals that do become principled and powerful.

Fundamentally changing an organizational culture is likely to take at least seven years. In most organizations seven years is forever. Almost everything can and usually does change in seven years. Cultural transformation must be accelerated if it is to be successful. The Shingo Model and the key concepts above may, with exemplary leadership, be reduced to four or five years! It's still not fast or easy.

I once worked with a wonderful company that upon hearing this message decided they were capable of focusing only on two or three things at a time. Ultimately, they selected three principles they felt were most critical to them and decided that these would become their organizational focus. Keeping track of more than three was just too much; "stick to the knitting" had become their motto.

A year or so later, the leadership team began to notice that while some progress had been made in some areas, in others they continued to experience poor results. To understand the cause for this, we worked backward from the poor results to understand what principle governed the creation of the outcomes they had expected to see. To their surprise, they discovered that these outcomes were heavily influenced by the principles they had decided not to focus on. They learned that principles always effect outcomes. By ignoring the principles that governed these specific results, the leaders of this company left themselves vulnerable to the consequences of their lack of attention. The principles were always in effect.

The old notion of picking a few things and being really good at them works for some things, but not when trying to understand, predict and control the creation of ideal results. A leader must be capable enough to consider all of the principles that have the greatest impact on an important outcome they are accountable to deliver.

A key manager came to me in private once and wanted to know how she could accelerate the transition of people's ability to understand and apply principles to their daily work. She told me that they had held study groups, read books, conducted workshops, and organized targeted coaching sessions but still felt like they were not really getting it. As I listened to her I remembered what John Schook had said to me many years ago, that it is much easier to act your way into a new way of thinking than it is to think your way into a new way of acting! How right he was!

My recommendation to the young manager was to put a principle to the test by implementing it. I told her to evaluate every key management and work system to make sure they were enabling behaviors consistent with the principle in question, especially top management behaviors, then consciously observe changes in results that would likely be connected with having implemented the principle. I suggested that she give it time and their absolutely best effort, then discuss with every affected person the cause and effect relationship between the principle and the results.

This experiment provided the experiential learning that changed minds and values. People came to value the principle and hence gain a natural desire to align their own behaviors. This is how a culture changes, one principle at a time, one person at a time, over time.

This is how a culture changes, one principle at a time, one person at a time, over time.

When a leader is guided by principles and the principles become a part of every associate's value system, people become powerful. I was taught once that powerful organizations are made up of powerful teams and powerful teams are made up of powerful people. My extension to this wisdom is that powerful people are people who know the principles that govern their success and live by them.

Powerful people are people who know the principles that govern their success and live by them.

Empowered employees become powerful not simply by having work delegated to them that was previously done by someone else. People become powerful when they have the information, knowledge and skills required to do the new work. Essential to what they must know are the principles that govern the work they are being asked to do. Because they are at the *Gemba*, they become the best prepared and most powerful people in making the day-to-day decisions that affect them.

Principles become the *why* for their actions. When people know *why*, they are capable of evaluating options and making informed decisions. This is how to ultimately empower people. When empowerment happens by teaching principles, leaders can go home earlier and spend fewer weekends in the office making sure that everyone does the right thing.

TUNE PRINCIPLES IN

A Sunday school teacher once told me that God's voice was always out there waiting to be heard. She likened it to an old-time radio with a dial for tuning in stations. I think she even used the old Norman Rockwell picture of the family gathered around the radio trying to tune in something important. She said if you want to hear the voice of God, you must first tune in.

I think her advice works perfectly for principles. If you want to hear the voice of a principle, you must first do the hard work of preparing yourself to hear them. You must tune them in through appreciative inquiry, application, personal experience, being willing to see reality and be vulnerable enough to learn and change your behaviors, no matter how hard.

A few years ago, I finally did something about not being able to hear my wife and got a new pair of hearing aids. The audiologist was so excited to explain the newest technology that allowed me to have a setting that would tune down the voices of others I didn't want to hear and amplify the voice I was trying to listen to. Wow! What a concept!

Learning to effectively hear the voice of principles requires us to turn down the many voices that would draw us back to the way we may have always done things and amplify the voice of principles that will guide us to new thinking, new beliefs and ultimately ideal behaviors and results.

Unlike my hearing aids that work on my tympanic nerves, principles speak to the nature of people. You have seen that each of the foundational truths that made the principles universal and timeless were about people and the nature of people. This is the main reason I have experienced so much fulfillment for the last ten years; because people do not hear principles with their ears or their heads, they hear or rather feel them in their hearts. Principles resonate inside of people. I routinely find myself putting my hands over my heart when I am explaining a principle. It is not a technique that leads to this action; it is a feeling.

People do not hear principles with their ears or their heads; they hear or rather feel them in their hearts. Principles resonate inside of people.

I remember where I was the day I first felt some of the principles that were a part of Total Quality Management. It was at a conference organized by the American Management Society at the Waldorf Astoria Hotel in New York City. I don't remember who the speaker was, but I remember the gestalt I experienced as the speaker talked about *Assuring Quality at the Source* and *Creating Value for Customers*. He used different words but was describing the same principles. After the session was over, a group of us met to have dinner and it was as though we had just come from a revival and all been born again. Once we had heard the voice it became impossible to deny its validity. This personal "ah ha" moment is what I hope for every seeker of the voice of principles.

AVOID DIFFUSION...MAKE IT "YOUR" CULTURE

Early in this book I described how after being conquered, the practices of one civilization were often adopted by the other. Typically what anthropologists have observed is that the adopted practice is short-lived apparently because the adopter was far more interested in the behavior than they were the reasons why the behavior was created in the first place. In other words they had learned the what and the how, but they had never taken the time to understand and embrace the thinking and beliefs behind it, the why.

> *Organizations often learn the what and the how, but often do not take the time to understand and embrace the thinking and beliefs behind it, the why.*

This phenomenon of diffusion accounts for much of the lack of sustainability in improvement efforts of companies over the last 50 years. Exciting new tools and practices are attractive, especially when they come with the promise of a quick payback.

Continuous improvement must become a vital part of every organization but it can never happen by simply copying the practices of someone else. Continuous improvement is a mindset that must be built into the beliefs and behaviors of every single person. The voice of principles answers for people the question of *why* and creates sustainability. Principles explain why we should do what we do. Knowing deeply the reason why something is right empowers people with the knowledge and ability to evaluate options, weigh consequences, decide with surety and act with confidence.

> *Knowing deeply the reason why something is right empowers people with the knowledge and ability to evaluate options, weigh consequences, decide with surety and act with confidence.*

In the absence of a principle people create bureaucracy. Bureaucracy is what is created to help people know what to do when they can't act for themselves.

Teaching people to listen to the voice of principles reduces waste, improves quality and speeds everything up. When people begin to evaluate all of the barriers to the continuous flow of value to customers, much of what they will confront is bureaucracy. As a leader you get the great job of stripping away the bureaucracy as you see people becoming powerful by listening to the voice of principles.

In the absence of a principle people create bureaucracy.

CONCLUSION

It was probably the wisdom of Solomon in the book of Proverbs that said, "Where there is no vision, the people perish." Principles create a vision of ideal that inspires and motivates people to want to move toward them. People may not perish from the lack of principles but they certainly might perish under the weight of the bureaucracy created to govern the unprincipled.

So now think about where you want to work every day. What kind of a culture do you think others want to be a part of? How many ping pong tables would you trade for the opportunity to self-govern and know that you are really making a difference in something everyone is committed to and aligned with? How many football tickets would it take to get you to leave a place where you felt respected and were given opportunities to develop your full potential as a human being? How many free power bars in the kitchen would you exchange for the fulfillment that comes from being listened to and then implementing your own ideas for how to make something better.

Sustainable cultures of excellence grounded in principles create incredible places for people to work and thrive and result in a continuous flow of value to customers.

Principles have a voice. These are the natural laws that govern the success of all of our business and organizational ventures. Principles speak the truth all day long, every day. Principles never take vacations or become irrelevant. Principles govern our results whether or not we pay attention to them. They shout to the person that has learned to listen and are mute to those who tune them out. The most successful people through the ages are those that are intimately familiar with the voice of principles and have become what we might call "principled."

Enterprises of all kinds and in every corner of the world are crying out for principled leaders and there is almost no end to the good that a leader that listens to the voice of principles can do. Perhaps you have already begun to hear their voices, if not, I invite you to consider the realignment of your values by tuning out the voice of your old paradigms and amplifying the voice of the principles.

Listen carefully. Can you hear them?

References

Barker, J. A. 1993. *Paradigms: The Business of Discovering the Future.* HarperBusiness.

Collins, J. C. 2001. *Good to Great: Why Some Companies Make the Leap... and Others Don't.* HarperBusiness.

Covey, S. 1989. *7-Habits of Highly Effective People.* Free Press

Deming, W. E. 1986. *Out of the Crisis.* Cambridge, MA: Massachusetts Institute of Technology, Center for Advanced Engineering Study.

DePree, M. 1987. *Leadership Is an Art.*

Ford, H. and Crowther, S. 1926. *Today and Tomorrow.* The Bookman (U.K.).

Rogers, C. 1980. *A Way of Being.* Houghton Mifflin Company

Index

Page numbers followed by f indicate figures.

Printed in the United States
by Baker & Taylor Publisher Services